Publisher and Creative Director: Nick Wells
Project Editors: Sara Robson and Cat Emslie
Art Director: Mike Spender
Digital Design and Production: Chris Herbert
Layout Design: Vanessa Green
Copy Editor: Mary-Ann Gallagher
Proofreader: Alexandra Davidson
Indexer: Helen Snaith

Special thanks to: Chelsea Edwards, Polly Prior and Jordi Nolla; and to
Hoonie Feltham for project management of the photographic shoot.

All photographs are © Foundry Arts.
All photographs are courtesy of Hugh Palmer, except the following:
Ged Palmer: 9, 13, 16, 17, 27, 32–34, 35 r, 36–37, 42, 45 cl, 58, 61, 70–71, 79 r, 80–82, 90–91, 146–47, 150, 158, 160–61,
163, 167, 172, 183 r, 186, 187 r, 187 cl, 192–93, 196, 199, 202–03, 205, 206, 207–08, 209 r, 222–23, 226–27, 238, 240, 245 b & t.
Iria Prol: 6 t, 7, 8, 10, 11, 12, 14 l & r, 15, 20–21, 26, 28–29, 30, 31, 35 l, 38, 39, 40–41, 43, 44, 45 r, 60, 78, 79 l, 87, 92 l,
93, 98–99, 114, 144, 145 r, 159, 162, 164–65, 173, 184–85, 194–95, 197, 204, 224, 225.

HUGH PALMER (author and photographer) is one of the world's leading photographers of landscape,
architecture and gardens. His work has been published in many magazines and reviews, including *Harpers
& Queen*, *Country Life* and *World of Interiors*. He has also carried out a host of book commissions
including *The Secrets of Venice*, published by Flame Tree, and many titles in the *Most Beautiful Villages*
series, published by Thames & Hudson. His photographs have also featured in Flame Tree's
The Secrets of Tuscany, *The Secrets of Provence* and *The Secrets of the Greek Islands*.

Fall River Press
122 Fifth Avenue
New York, NY 10011

ISBN: 978-1-4351-1933-8

Printed and bound in China

1 3 5 7 9 10 8 6 4 2

Barcelona

City of Dreams

Barcelona

City of Dreams

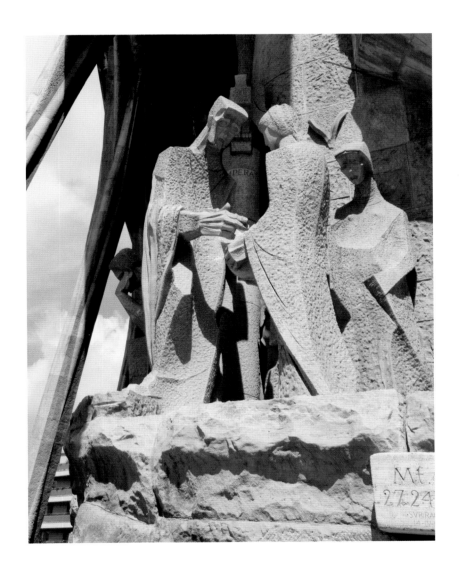

Author and Photographer: **HUGH PALMER**

FALL RIVER PRESS

CONTENTS

INTRODUCTION

Barcelona is very much a city that lives for the moment. It attracts a constant stream of visitors throughout the year, including a high percentage of younger people, drawn by the city's reputation as the happening 'party capital' of Europe. But after an all-nighter in one of the ultramodern, state-of-the-art nightclubs, party-goers might find themselves staggering home down a cobbled alley in a medieval quarter that has scarcely changed in 700 years. How can a city so bursting with contemporary energy simultaneously maintain such a profound contact with its past? The truth is that Barcelona's current artistic explosion, and the dramatic revitalization of its architectural fabric, are just the latest chapters in a long tradition of innovation. Progressive, radical Barcelona has always been the vanguard of Spain – not at the centre, but very much at the edge, tangential, sometimes even a thorn in its side. It has always looked outwards, across the Mediterranean or over the Pyrenees to France.

A brief glance at Barcelona's history will show that the roots of the city's proud independence and passionate regional identity run deep. The Roman town of Barcino was founded at the time of Caesar Augustus (63 BC–AD 14) in the first century BC; ancient ruins can still be made out in the Barri Gòtic, Barcelona's Gothic Quarter, which later grew up over the Roman settlement. The earliest fortifications were built to protect against raiders who came from beyond the Pyrenees to the north. But the biggest danger came from the south: the Moors invaded Spain in 711 and rapidly advanced northwards into France. They were pushed back over the Pyrenees by the Franks, leaving this north-eastern corner, a region which would soon become known as Catalonia, as the limit of the new Muslim territory. The Franks reconquered the area in 801 and Barcelona became a frontier town ruled by the *Comtes*, the Count overlords of the southern periphery of the Frankish empire. The first Catalans lived in the mountains to the north, which is how their language, similar to *langue d'Oc* (the lingua franca of post-Roman southern France) came into the area. In 985 the Moors attacked again, but this time the Franks failed to come to Barcelona's aid and the city had to fend for itself. Catalonia, of which Barcelona was already de facto capital, became self-determining and declared its independence.

In 1137, Count Ramon Berenguer IV (*c.* 1113–62) married Queen Petronella (1137–62), heiress of Aragon, making Catalonia part of a joint-state called the Corona d'Aragó (Crown of Aragon). This newly powerful state began to expand east across the Mediterranean, as successive Count-Kings developed trade links and conquered key territories. King Jaume I (1243–1311) managed to subdue the islands of Mallorca and Ibiza, as well as Valencia on the Spanish mainland. His son, Jaume II (1262–1327), took Sicily, Menorca, Malta, Gozo and even – albeit briefly – Athens. Attempts to take over Corsica and Sardinia were less successful but, during the fourteenth and fifteenith centuries, Barcelona was certainly the dominating trading presence in the western Mediterranean. During this time, the great palaces and churches of the Barri Gòtic and La Ribera were built.

But the expense of waging war and administering a vast empire gradually exhausted the resources of the Catalan state, which was also facing competition from the growing Ottoman Empire in the eastern Mediterranean. The Black Death arrived in 1348, killing a third of Barcelona's population; from 1400, the population declined to less than a third of that of its great rival Valencia.

When Ferdinand of Aragon (1452–1516) married Isabel of Castile (1451–1504) in 1479, it was hoped the union would bring much-needed finance to Barcelona. Instead, their gift to Catalonia was the unpopular inquisition in 1487. Power was concentrated in Castile, and Catalonia was deliberately marginalized. The departure of the Jews, expelled from Spain in 1492, had an adverse effect on Barcelona's economy, compounded when the region was specifically banned from lucrative trade routes with South America. During the following centuries, Catalans attempted (unsuccessfully) to throw off the repressive Castilian yoke many times, notably in the mid-seventeenth century, and again at the beginning of the eighteenth century during the War of Spanish Succession, when the Catalans backed Austrian Archduke Charles's (1685–1740) claim to the throne against Philip V (1683–1746). Barcelona was besieged for 15 months, and finally fell in 1714. This time, the Castilians hit back hard

Barcelona's population exploded from 115,000 at the start of the nineteenth century to half a million by the turn of the twentieth century. By 1930 it had reached one million. Only the rich could afford to move out to the new Eixample, and the poor were stuck in the miserable tenements of the old city. Conditions for the workers who had fuelled the city's industrial revolution remained appalling, and Barcelona became a centre for anarchist violence. Primo Rivera (1870–1930), who briefly declared himself dictator of Spain during the 1920s, tried to take on the Catalan nationalists and trade unionists but the repression simply fuelled Catalan radicalism. When the Spanish Civil War broke out in 1936, Barcelona was run by an Anarchist-Marxist coalition for a year, and became the national capital of the Republicans in the autumn of 1937. The Nationalists, led by General Francesco Franco (1892–1975), finally defeated the Republicans in 1939.

The years immediately following the end of the Civil War were especially hard for Catalonia, which was treated with particular brutality by the repressive and strongly centrist Franco government. Franco's efforts to repress the Catalan identity – not the first in Barcelona's history – were more savage and determined than any they had suffered previously. Thirty-five thousand Republicans were executed by the Fascist death squads between 1939 and 1941 alone. Despite aggressively pursuing policies designed to cement the Francoist vision of a single unified Spain, it proved impossible to stifle the Catalan identity. After Franco's death in 1975, Barcelona immediately reversed these policies: the Via Generalissimo Franco became Avinguda Diagonal once again, and Catalonia, among all the newly decentralized regions, became the leading activist in the anti-centrist lobby. The struggle to reassert Catalan identity is still evident everywhere: all local government proceedings are in Catalan, and it is the primary language in schools and universities. Catalan appears first on road signs and notices, with Spanish and English equal second.

The decision to host the 1992 Olympics in Barcelona was a great coup, which attracted massive funding and kickstarted the huge (and ongoing) civic expansion

at the recalcitrant Catalans; Philip V built a huge fortress (where the Cuitadella Park now stands) to watch over Barcelona from close quarters, and Catalan language and culture were vigorously suppressed.

By the end of the eighteenth century, the outlook was brightening for Barcelona. The ban on transatlantic trade with South America was lifted, and the city's manufacturing industry, particularly the production of textiles, started to expand. Barcelona industrialized rapidly, and the proliferating cotton mills gained it the nickname 'the Manchester of Spain'. The first railway line in Spain was built here in 1848, linking the city with Mataró. Barcelona, still squeezed into its medieval walls, grew increasingly cramped. Finally, in 1850, Barcelona was given permission to demolish the walls, and the city exploded outwards. An airy new Eixample (which means 'extension' in Catalan) was laid out on an elegant grid plan from 1854, and Barcelona's new-found wealth sought expression in the exuberant mansions of the industrialists. These were built in the fashionable Modernista style, which was the local interpretation of Art Nouveau, brought from Paris and transformed into something uniquely Catalan.

programme, which rivals the city's great reinvention of the mid-nineteenth century. Barcelona has a history of generating grandiose projects, from the Universal Exhibition of 1888 to the 1992 Olympic Games and the 2004 Universal Forum of Cultures. Each of these events has been used as an excuse to transform another neighbourhood, all rebuilt with Utopian vision and trademark panache.

Barcelona is the centre of Catalan government: the noble edifices of the Generalitat (Catalan parliament) and the Ajuntament (City hall) face each other across the ancient square of Sant Jaume, the Catalan flag flying proudly above their grand facades. A smaller office building in a nearby residential district bears a discreet plaque declaring it to be the Office of the Madrid Government. In what other regional city in the world could one see what looks like an embassy representing the interests of the national government?

Although Barcelona is the capital not of a state but of a small region, it nevertheless has always had the pretensions of a national capital. Its grand boulevards – among them, the Gran Via de les Corts Catalanes, the Avinguda Diagonal and the Passeig de Gràcia – resemble, in scale and pretension, the avenues of other great European capital cities such as Paris, London and Vienna, where the grand architecture was designed to reflect the power and prestige of a worldwide empire. Barcelona's achievements are fiercely localized, but its pride is on a global scale.

This is certainly like no other city in the world, and its citizens are passionate about celebrating its difference. They seem in a constant state of excitement; particularly since the repressive hand of Franco was lifted by his death, they have not stopped celebrating. The energy is palpable, and the city's present transformation is just the latest in a long and continuing series of exuberant reinventions.

WATERFRONT BARCELONA

Medieval visitors to Barcelona often described the city as '*oberta al mar*' ('open to the sea'), an apt description of a port whose fleets were starting to dominate Mediterranean trade, but inaccurate physically: lacking a natural harbour, the ancient quarter of La Ribera (meaning 'the shore') had to suffice. The increasing wealth and prestige of the Catalan merchants was expressed in the construction of the fourteenth-century church of Santa Maria del Mar, a Gothic masterpiece that still dominates La Ribera. Barcelona lost its medieval trading pre-eminence, but the port was revitalized from the late eighteenth century when transatlantic routes were reopened.

By the 1900s, the port was past its prime; its crumbling docks and warehouses lay idle, surrounded by rubbish dumps and disused railway sidings.

In preparation for the 1992 Olympic Games there was a giant clean-up. The docks of Port Vell (the old port) were transformed into a glamorous marina, and a broad boulevard was constructed to connect it with the Olympic Village, where 15,000 competitors were housed in apartments later made available for local residents. The previously grubby seafront was replaced with six sandy beaches, and the waterfront became one of the city's favourite playgrounds. The traditional eighteenth-century quarter of Barceloneta, a wedge-shaped grid jutting into the harbour, was designed to re-house fishermen and factory-workers, and retains its authentic charm. It still has a fishing village atmosphere and is popular with locals and visitors alike for its fresh seafood restaurants.

PORT VELL

Barcelona's old harbour, Port Vell, which stretches from the Columbus Monument to Barceloneta, has much to offer, from the relics of the city's maritime past to the up-to-date facilities and attractions offered by its recent redevelopment.

Honouring an Explorer

The huge statue of Christopher Columbus (1451–1506, *see* pages 14 and 15) was placed on top of his column for the World Exhibition in 1888; although not a native Barcelonin (in fact he was born in Italy), this monument was erected here because he certainly visited Barcelona at least once. The iron column is completely covered

with allegorical figures, while around the base a series of reliefs depicts important stages in Columbus's life and his voyages of discovery. The 8 m-high statue (26 ft) on top of the column points out to sea: not, as the artist intended, towards the New World, but towards the Mediterranean, which after all was the location of Catalonia's empire, if not Spain's.

Monumental Vistas

A lift takes visitors up inside the 51 m-high (167 ft) cast-iron column to emerge at the explorer's feet, where a vertiginous viewing gallery offers terrific views along the coastline: towards the Olympic harbour and the new Forum development in one direction, and Montjuïc, topped by a fort, in the other. At the foot of the monument, in the Portal de la Pau, horse-drawn carriages offer tours of the area. From the dockside, the *golondrines*, old-fashioned pleasure boats, depart every half-hour for a tour around the harbour.

Ship-building Prowess

If you skirt the imposing bulk of the Duana Nova (New Customs House), an over-ornate wedding cake of municipal importance thrown up in 1902, and head for the Drassanes Reials, you will find among the finest

examples of civilian Gothic architecture anywhere, these are the largest and best preserved medieval shipyards in the world. They have stood here for 800 years, and used to sit right on the water's edge. In their time, the Drassanes, where teams of skilled shipwrights once produced galleys, rivalled the great Arsenale of Venice. They have now been beautifully restored and are dedicated to the museum of Catalonia's proud maritime history.

Maritime Marvels

A recent acquisition for the museum has been a handsome three-masted schooner, the *Santa Eulàlia*, which dates from 1908. It was originally called the *Carmen Flores* but was later renamed after the city's patron saint. The ocean-going schooner used to make the run between Barcelona and Cuba; it has been fully restored and is open to visitors. Much of Port Vell is built on land reclaimed from the sea. To reach the giant retail and leisure complex of the Moll Espanya, a walkway runs seawards from the dock. This undulating wooden footbridge is called the Rambla del Mar (*see* page 21), and puts a modern twist on the traditional idea of a promenade. As well as a giant shopping centre named Maremagnum, the Moll Espanya houses an Imax cinema with three screens, and the Aquàrium, one of Europe's biggest marine leisure and education centres. It specializes in the study of Mediterranean sea life and is home to more than 11,000 marine animals of 450 different species, together with 5,000,000 litres of sea water to make them feel at home.

World Trade Center

The imposing circular structure that looms across the water to the right of the Rambla del Mar is Barcelona's new World Trade Center (*see* page 21), a 48-storey building designed by I.M. Pei (b. 1917), the celebrated Chinese-American architect responsible for the famous glass pyramid at the Louvre Museum in Paris, as well as the fabulous new Museum of Islamic Art in the Gulf Emirate of Qatar. As well as offices and conference facilities, the new centre includes a large hotel, part of Barcelona's drive to become the

biggest container port capital in the Mediterranean, as well as its busiest cruise ship destination.

The enormous metal towers (below, on the right) by the World Trade Center are supports for the spectacular cross-harbour cable car. This begins at the Torre San Sebastià at the end of Barceloneta's newly extended spit, and stops near the World Trade Center (Torre Jaume I) before sweeping upwards across the water to terminate on the northeast side of Montjuïc. A walk along the Moll de la Fusta gives an opportunity to ogle the glamorous yachts in the busy marina at Port Vell. On this wide promenade there is plenty of space for large-scale artworks, including the suitably polychromatic sculpture *Cap de Barcelona* (Barcelona Head, 1992, *see* page 16), by the pop artist Roy Lichtenstein (1923–97).

SANTA MARIA DEL MAR

Although the neighbourhood of La Ribera lays claim to the great Gothic basilica of Santa Maria del Mar, the church really belongs to the city's waterfront. La Ribera (which means the shore) was Barcelona's original port area (the coastline has shifted east over the centuries), which is why the Llotja (exchange) was built here as the city's first trading centre for the shipping merchants. Before the basilica was built, this was the site of a small church dedicated to Santa Maria d'Arenys (of the sand), as it was so close to the sea.

Harmony in Composition

Barcelona began this impressive church in the mid-fourteenth century in thanksgiving for the successful

subjugation of Sardinia; it took only 55 years to complete, which is why the architectural features work together to create such a harmonious whole.

Catalan Gothic Treasure

The giant, uncluttered interior of Santa Maria del Mar was designed without a transept; unlike the Gothic churches being built in other parts of Europe, where the impression of height was intensified by the narrowness of a space, the Catalan style was to attempt to create great width as well as height. This required particularly ingenious design and construction – the wider the roof span, the more liable it was to collapse. There are two aisles either side of the nave, but such is the delicacy of the perfectly proportioned columns, which soar up to a fan-vaulted ceiling, they do nothing to diminish the effect of a single space.

Cleansing Fire

It is partly because of the destructive efforts of some anticlerical anarchists that we can get such a good sense of this supreme achievement of Catalan Gothic architecture. In 1936 they set fire to the church – the resultant 11-day blaze, while mercifully sparing the overall structure, removed all the fussy Baroque clutter acquired over centuries. An additional bonus for the unadorned space is that it has the most wonderful acoustics – the church is full every Easter for a performance of Mozart's *Requiem*, and at Christmas for Handel's *Messiah*.

BARCELONA

Exploring this friendly, traditional neighbourhood – especially on a sunny morning when locals sit out on the streets and squares to enjoy the sunshine, and the enticing aromas of frying seafood waft through the air – it is easy to forget that the first community to arrive here did so in grim and tragic circumstances. The year 1714 was a particularly bitter one for Barcelona. The Catalans backed the losing side in the War of Spanish Succession (1701–14), and, in 1713, an irate Philip V (1683–1746) sent his troops to besiege the city, which fell after an heroic 15-month ordeal. The prospect of independence, always so close to Barcelona's heart, seemed at its most remote.

A King's Repression

In a vengeful move to dissuade the locals from future uprisings, the king ordered that a fort be built – the

notorious Ciutadella, which stood where the present Parc de Ciutadella is now laid out. Half of the district of La Ribera was torn down, and the 5,000 evicted residents were forced to demolish their own homes. Building land was scarce at the time, and the city was forbidden to expand northwards. A build-up of silt against the harbour dyke that protected

Port Vell had, during the previous century, given rise to a triangular-shaped area of natural landfill. So, in the 1750s, the military engineer Juan Martín Germeño was given the job of clearing away the shanty town that had developed there, and laying out a new residential district to house 10,000 fishermen, port-workers and sailors.

Living at Close Quarters

The small-scale grid pattern looks delightful to the visitor now, but Barceloneta must have been an infernally crowded place back when it was at its maximum capacity – particularly after many of the two-storey cottages specified in the original design were later converted to four- and five-storey tenements. Sharp-eyed visitors may be able to pick out some of the original dwellings.

Beach Life

The neighbourhood has managed to retain much of its original, salty character, with village life going on here independently of the bustling city. It is even more like an island now, however: the areas that surround it have changed drastically, and this is especially apparent during the summer months. Barceloneta's beach is one of the liveliest and most popular in the city, both during the day, when it is packed with sun-worshippers, and at night, when everyone flocks to the *xiringuitos*, beach bars located right on the sand.

Main Street Museum

Barceloneta's main street, the Passeig Joan de Borbò, starts at the Palau de Mar building (a former warehouse), which houses the Museu d'Història de Catalunya (Museum of Catalan History). The permanent exhibition here begins with prehistory, and covers the industrial revolution, the dictatorship and the current democratic system. The terrace of the museum café has an excellent observation deck, with views onto the neighbourhood and port.

New Role for Lighthouse

Close to the museum, and next to the Moll dels Pescadors, stands the Torre del Rellotge (Clock Tower). This is the area's oldest surviving structure, dating back to 1772. It served as the harbour's lighthouse until the middle of the nineteenth century but, when the harbour was modernized, it was no longer required. Locals did not want to pull it down, so it was decided to change its function to that of telling the time. At

around 5 pm, you may see fresh fish being auctioned off on the quay, after the small fishing fleet has returned to harbour.

Traditional Charm

From this point, down towards the beach, the neighbourhood really shows off its traditional character: balconies are festooned with washing drying in the sun and there is a wide choice of *bodegas*, bars and restaurants, including some of great renown, such as the century-old Can Solé (left). Barceloneta is definitely the best place to eat fresh fish in all of Barcelona. If the crowds waiting to sit down and eat a full meal are making the hunger pangs unbearable, then a selection of tapas (*tapes* in Catalan) eaten at the bar will quickly hit the spot.

Barcelonata Tapas

The classic *tapa* eaten here is called *la bomba* ('the bomb'), consisting of a potato ball stuffed with meat and served with a choice of spicy sauce or the traditional accompaniment, *allioli* – a delicious mayonnaise-like mixture of garlic and olive oil. An even more traditional accompaniment is the glass of fresh cool beer that will be drawn from a barrel behind the bar.

VILA OLÍMPICA

It is hard to imagine that the area now occupied by the ultramodern development of the Vila Olímpica was, less than 20 years ago, a jumble of crumbling factories, warehouses, rubbish dumps and disused train yards. The huge seafront development was planned and completed in time for the 1992 Olympics, providing accommodation for 15,000 competitors and support staff, along with a new marina, from which most of the watersports events took place.

Complete Overhaul

But all this was only part of a much larger programme of urban regeneration, intended to transform this seaward end of the industrial quarter of Poblenou. The plan was controversial among the locals, not only because much of their old neighbourhood was bulldozed in the process, but also because they feared that they would be excluded from buying property as prices were driven up by well-heeled incomers. The grumbles of the local residents have been justified to some extent, as the Vila Olímpica has become in effect a wealthy suburb, and the demands of the car, catered for by its wide boulevards, are prioritized over the comfort of pedestrians.

Architectural Splendours

The new buildings of the Vila Olímpica were designed by the architectural team of Martorell, Bohigas, Mackay and Puigdomènech, who laid out the streets like a mega-version of Barceloneta and created the housing that would become more than 2,000 apartments after the Games had finished. There are some pleasant green areas which break up the housing plots. One of these is the Atlanta Garden, which is overlooked by a relic of Poblenou's industrial past: the giant chimney known as Can Folch. Nearby, on the Carrer Salvador Espriu, there is a handsome fountain, the result of a happy collaboration between the Canarian sculptor Juan Bordas and the architect Òscar Tusquets, a Catalan star who is used to working with famous artists, having formerly collaborated with Salvador Dalí (1904–89).

Olympic Legacies

The focus of the Vila Olímpica is the Port Olímpic, which is locally considered more of a lasting civic asset. It has 714 berths, which accommodate a constant stream of luxury and sporting yachts up to 30 m (98 ft) in length. In the Plaça dels Campions, replicas of the 257 medals awarded during the 1992 Olympic Games are set in the ground, and the handprints of many of the participating athletes have been immortalized in concrete, in the style of Hollywood stars.

Two signature skyscrapers have become representative of the Port Olímpic: inevitably known as the Twin Towers, they are but distant relations of each other architecturally, but share a common height, 153.5 m (504 ft), which makes them the tallest buildings in Spain. The one with the external metalwork is the luxurious Hotel Arts (*see* previous pages, left), which was designed by the architects Bruce Graham (b. 1925) and Frank Gehry (b. 1929), with 456 deluxe rooms looking out to sea. Next to the Hotel Arts is the Mapfre Tower (*see* previous pages, right), which was designed by Iñigo Ortiz and Enrique de León. This serves as an office building, with the bottom floor taken up by a shopping centre. At the base of the tower is the Plaça dels Voluntaris, with an enormous fountain at the centre.

Glittering Neighbourhood

Closer to the sea glistens another creation by the American architect Frank Gehry, a giant sculpture called *Fish*, 1992 (below). This distinctive work is built out of bronze-coloured metal plates that shimmer and change colour according to the light, in the same manner as his titanium-clad Guggenheim building in Bilbao.

A host of bars and restaurants line the promenade along the port, and at night this turns into one of the busiest partying venues in the city, with crowds drawn by cocktail bars, clubs and a glamorous casino.

OLD TOWN BARCELONA

The Barri Gòtic (Gothic Quarter) was built on top of the old Roman settlement. Few traces remain of Roman Barcino, but these are intriguing enough; they can be viewed in the basement of the Museu d'Història de la Ciutat (City History Museum). The narrow warren of the Barri Gòtic still exudes the atmosphere of a medieval city, with its graceful courtyards, once-grand

mansions and the tangle of narrow streets emerging into irregular cobbled squares. It is bounded to the south by the great tourist attraction of the Rambla, a long avenue that runs from the modern Plaça Catalunya to the west, down to the Port Vell.

La Ribera, north of the Barri Gòtic, was home to fishermen and sailors before the medieval boom in

maritime trade. During the boom, when Barcelona ruled a Mediterranean empire that stretched as far as Greece, the newly wealthy merchants constructed a string of fine palaces, some of which survive along the Carrer Montcada.

The district on the other side of the Barri Gòtic is very different. El Raval takes its name from the Arabic expression for 'an area outside the walls'. Monasteries and convents were established here in the middle ages, but from the eighteenth century it began to fill with factories and tenements, and later became infamous for disreputable goings-on. Now it is being gentrified, although there are still vestiges of its old raffish past.

MUSEU D'ART CONTEMPORANI

The Museu d'Art Contemporani de Barcelona (Museum of Contemporary Art, known as MACBA for short) gleams like a newly landed apparition from outer space amongst the gritty realities of the surrounding streets. This gleaming white gallery is the jewel in the crown of the proud new civic spaces that now adorn the previously rundown neighbourhood of El Raval. The American architect Richard Meier (b. 1934) responded to the challenge of revitalizing a rundown area

almost as successfully as his compatriot Frank Gehry (b. 1929, he of the bronze fish down by the Port Olímpic, *see* page 42), whose titanium-clad abstraction breathed new life into the grubby and unprepossessing downtown area of Bilbao some years ago.

Meier used the museum space to create a dialogue between the distinctly ancient urban fabric outside and the modern art inside. The museum overlooks an expansive paved square, the Plaça dels Àngels, which is named after the sixteenth-century Convent dels Àngels (now a contemporary design institution and gallery space), which flanks one side.

Smooth, Shining Minimalism

The museum is clad in white panels of enamelled steel, and the main facade is adorned with horizontal glass louvres that filter natural light. A voluptuous, curvaceous gallery for special exhibitions protrudes from the building at the eastern end of the main facade. Behind the transparent facade is a dramatic long ramp, which zig-zags up from the entrance hall and connects four floors of galleries. It is reminiscent of the famous curving ramps of the Guggenheim Museum in New York, and gives continuous views over the square below, which is usually animated by the exertions of the area's many skateboarders.

Well Chosen Collection

The collection offers a tour of the contemporary art scene since the end of the Second World War, mainly as expressed in Catalonia, although many international artists are also represented. There are several galleries of differing sizes, in which the permanent collection is shown in a series of rotating exhibitions. Abstract sculpture is particularly well represented, as well as new work by Spanish and Catalan artists using the latest in computer-generated and audiovisual media.

El Raval is proud to be on the cutting edge, and Meier's flagship creation is a great minimalist counterpoint to the lavishly decorated constructions of his Modernista predecessors in other parts of the city.

CENTRE DE CULTURA CONTEMPORÀNIA

The Casa de Caritat, an old convent building that later became El Raval's grim workhouse and lunatic asylum, has been transformed during the recent revamping of the area into the Centre de Cultura Contemporània de Barcelona (Barcelona Centre of Contemporary Culture, or 'CCCB'), which elegantly complements the MACBA next door. Its down-at-heel northern courtyard was transformed by the addition of a huge glass and steel wall, and the juxtaposition of modern with old creates a striking setting for the music and film events that are held here. It also hosts temporary art exhibitions, usually on an urban theme.

RAMBLA DEL RAVAL

The oldest, western part of the neighbourhood of El Raval has been revitalized by the handsome presence of the Museu d'Art Contemporani de Barcelona, built in 1996. Another cheerful new amenity much enjoyed by residents of all ages is the Rambla del Raval, a broad, tree-lined boulevard that was created by clearing away a whole block of tenements in 2000. A good place for an evening drink and a spot of people watching, it also hosts music events in the summer. Many of the new immigrants in this multi-ethnic neighbourhood have come from Pakistan, and they use the new space to indulge their passion for cricket.

SANT PAU DEL CAMP

The ancient area of El Raval, lying south of the Rambla, developed a character very different from the rest of the old city right from the beginning. Hospitals and monasteries were established here when it lay outside the city walls, and it also provided space for shanty towns inhabited by semi-vagrants who were not allowed to live inside the city. El Raval was finally enclosed in the fourteenth century, when the ancient walls were extended, and is now very much part of the city centre. Although recent efforts have been made to clear away some of the worst of the slum-dwellings, it still contains a high concentration of low-rent housing and attracts the city's poorer immigrants.

A Hidden Treat

It's all the more surprising to find, along the Carrer Sant Pau, a medieval gem of a church whose name, Sant Pau del Camp (St Paul of the Fields), is testament to the fact that this former Benedictine monastery once stood in surroundings very different from the present day. Now it

rubs shoulders with inner-city apartment blocks on one side and a sports centre on the other. It is the oldest surviving church in the city, and is of particular interest as that rarity in Barcelona: an original example of Romanesque architecture.

Foundations of the Monastery

Sant Pau is not only extremely old but also remarkably intact. The monastery was founded by the Benedictines in the tenth century, but their church was later destroyed during a Muslim raid. The son of Comte Guifré el Pilós (Count Wilfred the Hairy), legendary founder of Catalonia, is buried here, in a tombstone dated 911. It is possible to see remnants of the original, even older, structure, which were recycled in the capitals and bases of the marble columns around the doorway. The great age of the church is evident from the state of the weather-beaten

carvings of Christ, Saint Peter and Saint Paul that decorate the tympanum. Around the doorway are simple thirteenth-century carvings of fish, birds and faces, above which are symbols of the four evangelists in relief. Above all of this is a relief of the hand of God.

Medieval Gem

The church was rebuilt in the eleventh and twelth centuries in the shape of a Greek cross, with three apses, and is a plain, unadorned space. Painted wooden carvings of saints (*see* page 55) glimmer gently in the dim light admitted by the narrow arrow-slit apertures and the small rose windows high up in the central dome.

The perfectly preserved twelfth-century cloister is a cheerier affair, a miniature jewel containing a little green garden with a central fountain. Its Arabic-style arches are held up by slender columns arranged in pairs, with playful animals adorning the capitals.

LONDON BAR

The London Bar has been a landmark drinking establishment since it opened in 1909, undiminished in popularity since Picasso (1881–1973) and his cronies used to congregate here attracted by the raffish reputation of El Raval. It also counted Catalan artist Joan Miró (1893–1983), as well as celebrated visiting party animals such as Ernest Hemingway (1899–1961), among its patrons, and has managed to keep much of its original atmosphere by the simple expedient of saving money on its upkeep.

ELS QUATRE GATS

Diving off from the broad, respectable expanse of the Avinguda del Portal de l'Àngel, down the dark, narrow alley of Carrer de Montsió, it is a pleasant surprise to find oneself in the colourful interior of one of Barcelona's most famous and historic bohemian hang-outs – Els Quatre Gats ('the four cats').
This tavern, founded in 1897 by the painter Pere Romeu and three fellow artists, became the unofficial headquarters of the Modernista avant-garde.

LA RAMBLA

ost visitors make for the Rambla, Barcelona's most famous avenue, as soon as they arrive in Barcelona. Despite the inevitable crowds generated by such international celebrity, the long promenade still retains much of the irresistible charm that inspired the Spanish poet Lorca (1899–1936) to name it 'the most beautiful street in the world'. The year-round carnival show of human statues, buskers, street artists and musicians is always diverting.

From River to Road
Rambla is the Arabic word for 'sandy gully', and the avenue follows the course of a river that once ran down from the Golserolla mountains to the sea. When the city's first walls were built, their course was decided by the Rambla, which formed a defensive moat along their length. Inevitably it became a medieval sewer, earning the nickname of Gagallel, the 'turd-stream'.

Eventually it was filled in and later paved over; when it was further beautified in the nineteenth century, the plane trees planted here grew so well that Barcelonins joked that the less fragrant past of the Rambla was responsible.

Five Sections
There are actually five 'Rambles', distinct sections each with a different name, which together form one continuous walkway, with traffic limited to a narrow one-way lane on each side.

The Rambla de Santa Mònica starts off near the Monument a Colom (Columbus Monument) near the harbour. On the left, near the beginning of the street, is the Center d'Art Santa Mònica (CASM), a former convent that has been turned into an arts centre.

Rambla No. 2
Further up, the stately facade of the Gran Teatre del Liceu (*see* pages 72–77) dominates the Rambla dels Caputxins. On the opposite side, and a little way up, the eye-catching Modernista Casa Bruno Quadros was built in the 1890s as an umbrella shop, and its facade is studded with parasols and a huge oriental-style green dragon (below and right).

The dragon overlooks the little square called Pla de la Boqueria, with a pavement mural by Joan Miró, which adjoins the Rambla de Sant Josep. This stretch is lined with colourful flower stalls, which has given it the popular name of the Rambla dels Flors (below). On the left is the famous market of La Boqueria (*see* pages 66–71), and, further up, the Palau de la Virreina, a municipal exhibition space. Nearby is the sombre facade of the Església de Betlem, built for the Jesuits.

Colourful Diversion

The Rambla dels Estudis is better known as the Rambla dels Ocells ('the rambla of the birds') for the little stalls selling all kinds of birds, from canaries to chickens. Then comes the Rambla de Canaletes, named for its famous cast-iron fountain, a drink from which is supposed to ensure that you will come back to Barcelona. This section opens up onto the Plaça de Catalunya.

LA BOQUERIA

Almost every district of Barcelona has its own covered market, and the high gastronomic standards of the city owe as much to the outstanding quality of the produce they provide as they do to the flair of the Catalan cook. Each district claims that their market has the best produce, but you'll be spoiled for choice in any of them. The range and quality far exceeds the expectations of anyone unfortunate enough to be confined to shopping in the styrofoam-enclosed, plastic-wrapped, brave new world of the supermarket.

The largest and most central of Barcelona's markets is the Mercat Sant Josep, located halfway up the Rambla on the left. It is popularly known as La Boqueria (meaning 'goat meat market'), a name that may date back to the early thirteenth century, when tables were laid out by the old city gates to sell meat.

A Perfect Showcase

For centuries there was no enclosure, nor even a regular fixed market, on this spot: it was merely the extension of the line of stalls that ran from the Plaça del Pi along the present Carrer de la Boqueria. By the middle of the nineteenth century, when the Rambla de Sant Josep had taken on its present form, the city authorities decided to build an official covered market on this site. A design by the architect Josep Mas i Vila (1779–1855) was chosen and construction began in 1840, but plans were modified many times. The fish market was added in 1911 and three years later the stupendous Modernista metal roof that still covers the market today was completed.

As well as adding the required Barcelonin flair to the building, the roof (like its contemporary equivalent at the new Mercat Santa Caterina in La Ribera) provides the perfect balance of lightness and airiness for the comfort of shoppers and stallholders, ensuring that their produce is shown off to its best advantage.

GRAN TEATRE DEL LICEU

By the middle of the nineteenth century, worker discontent in Barcelona was coming to the boil. Booming industry had brought wealth to the merchants but not to the workers, who lived in increasingly desperate, miserable conditions. A series of more and more violent revolts broke out in the 1830s, during which several of the monasteries and convents that once lined the Rambla were burnt down. The land occupied by one of these unfortunate institutions was chosen as the site of a private opera house, erected thanks to subscriptions raised by the Sociedad Dramática de Aficionados. This demonstration of civic pride showed that the confidence of the merchants and industrialists remained undiminished despite the political turmoil.

Early Doors

The patience of the stallholders and their customers is stretched to the maximum by the army of tourists (drawn into the market by the visual delights of the food on offer) who clog the narrow walkways. Unfortunately they take little of it away except on the memory cards of their cameras. As with any serious market, the best time to come is in the early morning, particularly when the stallholders are just finishing arranging their displays: the early morning sun slants in, the squirmy piles of squid are at their glistening best and you can rub shoulders over *xocolata amb xurros* (hot chocolate and fritters) with traders, wholesalers, chefs and the bleary-eyed revellers of the late-night Rambla at the Bar Pinotxo, the most popular of the market's counter-bars.

GRAN TEATRE DEL LICEU

By the middle of the nineteenth century, worker discontent in Barcelona was coming to the boil. Booming industry had brought wealth to the merchants but not to the workers, who lived in increasingly desperate, miserable conditions. A series of more and more violent revolts broke out in the 1830s, during which several of the monasteries and convents that once lined the Rambla were burnt down. The land occupied by one of these unfortunate institutions was chosen as the site of a private opera house, erected thanks to subscriptions raised by the Sociedad Dramática de Aficionados. This demonstration of civic pride showed that the confidence of the merchants and industrialists remained undiminished despite the political turmoil.

The Resurrections

After an accidental fire burned the theatre down in 1861, an even larger version was constructed in its place, with a massive auditorium seating more than 2,000 spectators – second only in size to La Scala opera house in Milan. It truly deserved its new title: the Gran Teatre del Liceu.

But the opera-going classes were not to escape unscathed from the resentments of the dispossessed. In 1893 the auditorium was once again destroyed when an anarchist threw bombs during a performance of the opera *William Tell*, killing 22 people. And again, unfortunately, yet another fire destroyed the auditorium in 1994, but a campaign to replace it began immediately.

Best of Both Worlds

Five years later, the city had brought the Liceu (as it is universally known) back to life, although this time the carefully reconstructed nineteenth-century auditorium was equipped with the latest in computer technology. The theatre is now owned by the city, and has established a proud reputation as one of Europe's premier opera houses. It has also launched the careers of such homegrown operatic superstars as José Carreras (b. 1946) and Montserrat Caballé (b. 1933), both born in Barcelona.

Hidden Beauty

The theatre's main facade (left) overlooks the Rambla, and is surprisingly modest compared with the interior. Inside, a wide vestibule fringed with large columns leads to a great marble staircase built in 1861 (right), which is dominated by a Modernista sculpture by Venanci Vallmitjana (1826–1919) called *Al·legoria de la Música* (1901).

The staircase leads up to the Hall of Mirrors, a glorious room that was restored in 1877 by architect Elies Rogent (1821–97), and is elaborately decorated with gilded columns, huge mirrors and glittering chandeliers. Happily it was unscathed during the 1994 fire, and is once again in use as a foyer for opera-goers to take their intermission refreshments while admiring reflections of themselves in the tall mirrors or gazing at the grandiose frescoes on the ceiling. All is a sumptuous reflection of the grand pretensions of the original founders in the nineteenth century.

PALAU GÜELL

One of Antoni Gaudí's (1852–1926) earliest masterpieces is to be found, rather surprisingly, in the El Raval district, just off the southern part of the Rambla. His most important and faithful patron, the wealthy industrialist Eusebi Güell i Bacigalupi (1846–1918), commissioned Gaudí to build an annexe to his family residence on the Rambla. Even in this early project, the young architect displayed a daring sense of space and form, as well as an innovative use of traditional techniques, stretching the limits of everyday building materials and conventional construction methods. Most architects conceal the supports and structural frame of a building, but Gaudí found novel, even eccentric, ways to solve structural issues. He was constantly experimenting, and his unusual forms often derive their inspiration from nature. The extraordinary brick pillars (below and overleaf) that hold up the main house are visible in the basement (which was also used as the Palau's stables), forming a forest of mushroom-like columns that create an other-worldly atmosphere despite the humble, unfaced brick used in their construction.

A Happy Ending

The building had an unhappy function after the fall of Barcelona at the end of the Spanish Civil War in 1939. The Franco regime used it as a headquarters for their police activities, including the incarceration and torture of political prisoners in the basement. Extensive

renovations were completed in 2002, the 150th anniversary of Gaudí's birth. Unfortunately, these works uncovered structural weaknesses in the original stonework, and most of the palace remains closed while an ongoing restoration programme brings it up to the required standards of safety. The Palau Güell was one of the first buildings in the world to be chosen by UNESCO to be declared a World Heritage Site, and ensuring the building's future is a priority for the city.

CATEDRAL

The Barri Gòtic is dominated by the city's commanding cathedral, known in the local tongue as La Seu and dedicated to Barcelona's patron saint, Santa Eulàlia (c. 290–303). The current cathedral was begun in 1298 on the site of an old Romanesque building. A few stone reliefs from this earlier edifice are still preserved by the northeast doorway, the Portal de Sant Iu: one depicts the Catalan patron saint Sant Jordi (Saint George, c. 275–303) spearing the dragon, and another shows the city's first official ruler, Count Wilfred the Hairy, tussling with a griffon (below).

Late Additions and Unorthodox Features

Although most of the cathedral was completed by the mid-fifteenth century, the main facade, fancifully decorated in contrast to the austere interior, was only finally added in the 1880s. (This should give heart to

those who despair of Barcelona's other great church, Gaudí's enormous Sagrada Família, which is still a building site.) The layout of the cathedral is also rather unusual: the apse and altar area lie to the southeast whilst the main facade faces northwest.

A Gothic Masterpiece

The interior is a huge, soaring Gothic masterpiece, with a central nave flanked on either side by two aisles of approximately the same height, which are separated by rows of graceful, slender pillars. The side aisles are lined with chapels, most dating from the sixteenth and seventeenth centuries, which are decorated with elaborate baroque altarpieces. At the centre of the nave

is the Gothic choir, with exquisitely carved wooden stalls. Just in front of the main altar, a small staircase descends to a dim crypt, visible under a wide and low arch. This contains the marble tomb of Santa Eulàlia, who shares the honour of being Barcelona's patron saint with the Virgen de La Mercè.

Cloistered Oasis

For most visitors, the cloister of La Seu is the prettiest corner of the cathedral. The entrance, a short walk from the Plaça Sant Jaume, opens into a green, lush oasis, overlooked by magnolias and palm trees. The cloister was built between 1380 and 1451, and is lined with chapels dedicated to the patron saints of the city's medieval guilds. In the cloister garden is a small pond watched over by 13 vociferous geese (left): 13 because that was the age when Eulàlia met her unfortunate end, and geese because they did a good job as burglar alarms on the Capitoline Hill in Rome. In the middle of the pond, a fountain is crowned by a small statue of Sant Jordi (St George) with the dragon. During the feast of Corpus Christi, a hollow egg is set to 'dance' on the jet of the fountain in an ancient custom known as *l'ou com balla*.

PLAÇA DEL PI

A short stroll from the monumental Plaça Reial, a pair of adjoining, charming squares (the Plaça del Pi and the Plaça de Sant Josep Oriol) are overlooked by one of the old city's best-loved churches, Santa Maria del Pi (left). The name comes from the pines that once stood here, and a single tree still stands in the square in front of the church's main facade.

Enjoying the tranquility of this enclosed space over a coffee on one of the café terraces, it is hard to believe that the thronged Rambla lies less than a minute's walk away. The swirling sgraffito decoration that is found throughout the Barri Gòtic is demonstrated to good effect on the facade of the house that stands at number 3 Plaça del Pi (below and right). This is the city's earliest example of the art, and dates from 1685.

The Plaça Sant Josep Oriol, flanking the other side of the church, was named after a priest who looked after the parish here in the seventeenth century, and was canonized for his good works. An artists' market enlivens the square on Saturdays and Sundays.

PLAÇA DE SANT JAUME

The Plaça de Sant Jaume has always occupied an important position in the old city: before acquiring its present form, this was the site of the Roman Forum and marketplace. It is connected to the Rambla by the Carrer Ferran, one of the few streets in this part of the Barri Gòtic to allow cars.

Face to Face

Fortunately, the cars are allowed only limited access to the square, so visitors will be able to gaze upwards at the two great buildings that face each other across the square. On the eastern side, the Ajuntament (City Hall, below) was largely rebuilt in the nineteenth century; opposite, the Palau de la Generalitat (*see* page 92 right) is the ancient home of the Catalan government.

The latter's unremarkable Renaissance facade that it presents to the Plaça de Sant Jaume gives little sense of the rich architectural inheritance within.

The oldest section of the Palau de la Generalitat overlooks the Carrer del Bisbe and dates from 1418. A spirited depiction of Sant Jordi (St George, Catalonia's patron saint) slaying the dragon adorns a rondel, the work of Pere Joan (1413–82). It so delighted the authorities that the artist was paid double the agreed fee.

Overhead is a Bridge of Sighs (right), which was built in the run-up to the Universal Exhibition held in Barcelona in 1929. This walkway connects the Generalitat to the official residence of the Catalan President, the sixteenth-century Casa dels Canonges.

Sant Jordi (St George)

On St George's feast day, 23 April, the Generalitat is thrown open to visitors for the day (although visits are also possible on Sundays), and crowds flock to the stalls in the Plaça Sant Jaume to buy books and roses for their loved ones, in a local variant of the St Valentine's Day tradition.

PLAÇA DE GEORGE ORWELL

Catalonia has reason to be proud of its association with the radical British novelist George Orwell (1903–50). He came here in 1936, one of the many idealists who made a pilgrimage to Barcelona to join the Republican cause. He barely escaped with his life after he was wounded by sniper fire at the front, but managed to evade arrest before being smuggled out of the city. There is a small triangular square bearing his name just off the Carrer Escudellers, which has become a popular chilling-out spot for a young, alternative crowd.

PLAÇA DE SANT JUST

Tucked away behind the lofty classical Ajuntament is an enchanting little square whose irregular shape is typical of the higgledy-piggledy medieval layout of this part of the city. It is overlooked by the Església dels Sants Just i Pastor, thought to be the oldest church in the city, having been founded in 801, although the present Gothic construction dates to the mid-fourteenth century. In front of it is a well restored fourteenth-century fountain (below), which was donated to the city by Joan Fiveller, a merchant and councillor who lived on nearby Carrer del Lledó.

PLAÇA REIAL

The expansive Plaça Reial is curiously easy to miss, hidden behind an archway towards the seaward end of the Rambla. This is the city's only 'set-piece' square, laid out in the mid-nineteenth century and enclosed on all four sides by arcades, with a central fountain depicting the Three Graces. Its present elegance gives little clue of its dramatic beginnings: a Capuchin convent once occupied this site, but it was burnt down in 1835 by an enraged mob who had just witnessed a disappointing bull-fight held in honour of Queen Isabel's (1830–1904) birthday. The citizenry dragged the offending bull to the convent, and were whipped up to their incendiary frenzy by the street orators of those radical times.

A Model Square

The city authorities decided to use the land formerly occupied by the convent for a splendid new square. Local architect Francesc Daniel Molina chose Madrid's Plaza Mayor as a model, and designed a grandly neoclassical square, bordered by three-storey apartment buildings painted in harmonious pastel shades, topped by balustrades and decorated with busts of imperial explorers. The square may appear grand and aristocratic, but until comparatively recently it was badly neglected and the atmosphere was downright raffish. However, it has been beautifully restored and steps were taken to discourage the drug-dealers, hippies and down-and-outs in the 1990s.

Nowadays, tourists making for the numerous outdoor tables serving seafood and pizza far outnumber the few eccentrics who continue to linger here. On Sunday mornings, the last remnants of the all-night clubbing crowd mingle with the stallholders who come here to set up for the weekly stamp-and-coin market. The lamp posts that flank the central fountain are unusually exuberant, possibly because they are the earliest known work of a young man studying architecture in the city at the time: one Antoni Gaudí.

LOS CARACOLES

VIA LAIETANA

At the corner of Garrer Escudellers and Carrer Nou de Sant Francesc, an open brazier with rows of chickens turning on spits flames away every evening. It's a suitably old-fashioned way of advertising the presence of Los Caracoles, founded in 1835 and a celebrated landmark. The small front bar burrows inwards and downwards to a bewildering warren of small dining rooms, between which long-suffering and much-practised waiters stagger up and down bearing the dishes that emanate from a kitchen that looks like the innermost circle of Dante's (c. 1265–1321) 'Inferno'.

The Barri Gòtic is largely pedestrianized, and the few streets that are open to traffic are narrow and restricted. The busy Via Laietana, laid out in 1908, was intended to relieve the congested city centre and provide direct access to the waterfront. It slices down the natural boundary between the Barri Gòtic and La Ribera. During its construction, however, almost 2,000 houses were pulled down, and more than 10,000 residents were displaced, thus carving away a large part of the medieval Gothic centre of the city.

PALAU DE LA MÚSICA CATALANA

During the boom years of the nineteenth century, Catalan language and culture underwent a revival known as the *Renaixença*, or Renaissance. The tremendous new enthusiasm for Catalan traditions found its expression in many ways, including the formation of numerous choral groups among the workers. The most important of these was the Orfeó Català, founded in 1891. This choral group enjoyed such success and prestige that the celebrated Modernista architect Lluís Domènech i Montaner (1850–1923) was commissioned to build it a magnificent new home.

A Concentration of Extravagance

The Palau de la Música Catalana is an extraordinarily lavish building, completed in 1908, which was squeezed into a somewhat cramped site. The narrowness of the surrounding

streets means that it is necessary to crane upwards to admire the sumptuous facade (previous pages), where ornate floral mosaics adorn the columns, and flamboyant sculptural groups represent the spirit of Catalan popular music.

A Feast for the Senses

Inside, the foyer, supported by richly tiled columns, prepares the visitor (or concert-goer) for the splendours of the auditorium itself. This is found up a swirling staircase, where the building's leitmotif of flowers is expressed in every imaginable material. The red carpet leads into the main concert hall, a massive horseshoe arrangement of stalls and two dress circles, which can seat up to 2,000 patrons. The ceiling of blue-and-gold stained glass is adorned with a spectacular multicoloured skylight (left), designed by Domènech i Montaner and the glass-specialist Antoni Rigalt, which sceptics said was an engineering impossibility. A wild assortment of sculptures is clustered around the proscenium arch, including a bust of the composer Beethoven and several of Wagner's galloping Valkyries at full stretch. This almost

indigestible feast for the visual senses does come at a price: despite numerous attempts to improve the poor acoustics of the auditorium, it remains a better showplace for the home-grown musical tradition of Catalonia than the less strident subtleties of the classical repertoire.

'Palace of Catalan Junk'

The architect certainly delivered a full-blown fantasy of Modernista delights, but, not surprisingly, the project ran into financial problems. Domènech i Montaner was in too much of a fury about not being paid to attend the opening of the theatre, which took place only three years after construction commenced. Just 10 years later, changing fashions turned the city's arbiters of taste against this tribute to the Catalan *Renaixença*. It was denounced as an ostentatious monument, a 'Palace of Catalan junk'. But calls for its demolition were ignored and, now beautifully restored, it remains a glorious symbol of the heights of Modernista architectural decoration. It also provides a suitable setting for a wide-ranging concert programme, which runs the gamut from international jazz artists to Catalan choral concerts.

MERCAT DE SANTA CATERINA

The old centre of Barcelona boasts not one but two large food markets, testifying to the preference of its citizens for buying their produce fresh and of a quality superior to that found in a supermarket. Like the famous Boqueria market on the Rambla, the Mercat de Santa Caterina (which is located just across the Via Laietana from the great cathedral complex of La Seu) was built on the site of a demolished monastery, which is why, despite its very mercantile character, it bears such a pious name. The market is always thronged with locals, who mingle with the many immigrants from North Africa and Latin America who live in the closely packed residential streets in this northern section of La Ribera.

Endless varieties of seafood, poultry and cold meats, along with every kind of olive imaginable, tantalize the eye; try the celebrated market restaurant when the hunger pangs become too strong to resist.

Rejuvenated Building

The market building has recently had a very thorough facelift, to a design by Enric Miralles (1955–2000), the architect responsible for Scotland's much praised new parliament building, and his colleague Benedetta Tagliabue (b. 1963). It is a highly successful scheme that has retained many features from the original nineteenth-century design, and has even incorporated parts of the city's medieval walls, visible through glass panels. A generously lofty ceiling lined with slats of pale wood makes the enclosed area light and airy, and very pleasant to shop and work in. Above, the distinctive wavy form of its vivid polychrome tiled roof is reminiscent of the famous Modernista undulations to be marvelled at in the Park Güell. The supports for the roof are of an organic design that elegantly echoes the abundant fruit and vegetables on sale below. Giant bundles of grey steel 'tree trunks' soar upwards between the neatly spaced avenues that have survived from the market's original layout.

MERCAT DEL BORN

The Mercat del Born stands at the end of the long, narrow Passeig del Born, on the northern edge of La Ribera. Built in 1876, it is a cast-iron construction topped by a patent tile roof, which was designed by Josep Fontserè (1829–97), who also laid out the neighbouring Parc de la Ciutadella. Like many of Barcelona's historical buildings, it is in a state of transition. Its transformation into a cultural centre has been halted, however, while archeologists excavate the eighteenth-century ruins that have been uncovered during building works.

PALAU DELS MARQUESOS DE LLIÓ

The Palau dels Marquesos de Lló, which dates back to the thirteenth century, is one of the finest noble mansions to be found along the Carrer Montcada. It is part of the city's new Hub del Disseny (Design Hub), and functions as a research centre and temporary exhibition space, covering the disciplines of architecture and interior design, visual communication, product design and fashion. At the pretty courtyard café, refreshments can be enjoyed while admiring the gravity-defying Modernista 'hanging gardens' above (right).

LA RIBERA

In Roman times, the area that would later become known as La Ribera lay outside the city walls, and was sparsely dotted with villas and farm estates. By the thirteenth century, it was the heart of the city, and the most economically important district. Two distinct communities had grown up: to the north was Vilanova Sant Pere, clustered around the monastery of Sant Pere de les Puelles, while to the south, close to the sea front, was the Vilanova de Mar, built around the Romanesque church that would soon be replaced by the basilica of Santa Maria del Mar.

Mansion Courtyards

The area closest to the sea became the first commercial centre of Barcelona, and the increasingly wealthy merchants built their mansions and palaces along its narrow streets. The Carrer Montcada (left and below) was the smartest street of La Ribera during the

fourteenth and fifteenth centuries, and still holds the greatest number of these fine Gothic mansions, which are typically entered from the street by an archway that reveals a small courtyard, usually cobbled. From here an external stairway (*see* page 114) leads to the upper floor, where the merchant would live with his family while the business took place below. Five adjoining Gothic palaces now house the Museu Picasso, which honours the famous Andalusian artist who moved to Barcelona with his family when he was just 12 years old. La Ribera continued to be the commercial centre of Barcelona for

centuries, until much of the area was razed during the eighteenth century to make room for the vast fortress of the Ciutadella, and merchant trade began to be transferred to the new docks at Port Vell.

Artisanal Past

More than money was made in La Ribera. The tiny streets reveal the names of the artisans who once congregated here: Carrer de l'Argenteria (street of the silversmiths); Carrer Corders (rope-makers); Carrer Sombrerers (hat-makers); and (below) Carrer Flassaders (blanket-makers).

WESTERN BARCELONA

When the stately Avinguda Diagonal was extended westwards, it connected Barcelona to some formerly secluded country areas that were to become some of the city's most fashionable suburbs. Pedralbes, taking its name from the 'white stones' used in the construction of the fourteenth-century Monestir de Pedralbes, was the richest of these. Indeed, it can even boast a royal palace, first built for Gaudí's (1852–1926)

wealthy patron, Eusebi Güell (1846–1918), but later donated, rather uncharacteristically for Catalonia, to the Spanish royal family. Pedralbes is still a well-to-do residential neighbourhood with dignified avenues and luxurious apartment blocks.

Neighbouring Sarrià also nestles at the foot of the chain of hills that cut Barcelona off from inland Catalonia. Here, although the grand apartments with

doormen predominate, the centre of old Sarrià has small village-style squares. Sarrià is home to one of Gaudí's early masterpieces, the Col·legi de les Teresianes, a school that he completed in 1888.

Below Pedralbes, the neighbourhood of Sants has a more modest reputation. It grew up along the Carrer de la Creu Coberta, the old Roman road that runs into Barcelona from the west. Originally the community served those who arrived after the city gates shut at night. Now it's still one of the major gateways into the city, as it contains Barcelona's biggest train station. At one time this area was the industrial engine-house of Barcelona, and the avant-garde Parc de l'Espanya Industrial, next to the train station, was laid out in 1986, when a huge textile factory was demolished.

MONESTIR DE PEDRALBES

Queen Elisenda de Montcada was the fourth and final wife of Jaume II (1262–1327). She founded this convent for the Poor Clare Sisters in 1326, creating a cloistered haven of peace among what were then open fields. Although the surrounding area is now built up, the monastic complex, approached up a cobbled lane from the top of the Avinguda Pedralbes, retains its sequestered charm. The church and convent buildings are very similar in style, as they were all built at the same time, and present a complete picture of what monastic life was like 700 years ago. The community of nuns has moved to modern quarters nearby, and the monastery has been opened to visitors as part of Barcelona's city history museum.

Peaceful Corners

The delicious sense of peace is savoured most powerfully when exploring the magnificent three-storey cloister, with its triple rows of elegant, delicate columns (*see* page 123).

An immaculately kept garden (*see* page 125) preserves the traditional cross plan, and is planted with herbs, fragrant shrubs, fruit trees and cypresses, which are irrigated from the central fountain in the Arab

manner. One corner of the cloister is occupied by a baroque fountain enclosed by stone benches, forming a charming outdoor 'room'.

Quiet, Please

The visitor can explore the tiny cells where the nuns lived, as well as their kitchen, stables and storeroom. Adjoining the Cloister is the Capella de Sant Miquel (St Michael's Chapel), which has some outstanding Gothic frescoes

(1346) by Ferrer Bassa (*c.* 1285–1348). The austere refectory still has placards on its wall commanding obedience to the rule of silence, to be observed even when eating; a pulpit set into the wall gives a clue as to what was served up as an alternative to conversation.

Col·lecció Thyssen-Bornemisza

The dormitory, on the first floor, was home for some years to part of the superb Col·lecció Thyssen-

Bornemisza, an exceptional art collection that includes works by Fra Angelico (*c.* 1395–1455), Raphael (1483–1520) and Cranach (1472–1583); when Spain acquired the collection in the early 1980s, the Catalan wife of Barón Thyssen-Bornemisza (1921–2002) ensured some of its finest pieces went to Barcelona, although the bulk of the collection is on display in Madrid. The artworks have been moved to Barcelona's Palau Nacional, and the dormitory now displays a homely assortment of religious paintings and artefacts.

The Convent Church

A doorway leads from the pretty gardens in front of the monastery to the interior of the convent church, with a single nave lined on either side with chapels. The nave is divided by a wall and a delicate wrought-iron screen, which separate the general public from the convent community (this is still a closed order). In the church are some fine fifteenth-century stained-glass windows by Mestre Gil, and the alabaster tomb of Queen Elisenda, with a very lifelike sculpture commissioned just before her death in 1364.

PEDRALBES

During the nineteenth century, wealthy Barcelonins escaped to the cool hills around the city during the sticky summer months. The green hills of rural Pedralbes were especially sought-after, and numerous Modernista villas were erected. Only a handful of these have survived (left and above), dotted among the luxurious modern residences and apartment blocks that now characterize the neighbourhood. Modern Pedralbes remains one of the most elegant and desirable residential districts in the city.

SARRIÀ

Sarrià was only officially annexed to Barcelona in 1921, making it the last of the once-independent towns surrounding the metropolis to be swallowed up. It still retains a village feel in the narrow streets of its old centre, which is now considered among the most desirable residential quarters of Barcelona – quiet and rather exclusive. If one's apartment does not have the luxury of a private garden for enjoying the sunshine of a summer afternoon, there's always the balcony (this house, right, will undoubtedly have both).

PAVELLONS DE
LA FINCA GÜELL

The wealthy Güell family, Gaudí's most faithful patrons, owned several properties in Barcelona, including a country estate (*finca*) in the quiet hills of Pedralbes. A short walk from the Avinguda Pedralbes will bring you to the pavilions of the Finca Güell, designed by the young Gaudí in the 1880s. Eusebi Güell commissioned Gaudí to decorate the gatehouse as well as the gardens and the entrance to his summer home, at the same time as the architect was working on the Palau Güell in the old city. The two pavilions tucked inside the gateway are extraordinary, whimsical creations of brick and tile (left and above), but it is the gate itself that is the most imaginative feature (right). A terrifying winged dragon, constructed entirely from sheet metal and whiplash wrought iron, writhes across the gate. It seems to issue a playful threat to passers-by, warning them not to pass too close to its cruel bared teeth.

PARKS & GARDENS

Parc de Joan Miró

After the municipal abattoir (*escorxador* in Catalan) was pulled down to the east of the Sants district, the Parc Joan Miró (also known as Parc de l'Escorxador) was laid out in the 1980s. It sits next to Barcelona's Modernista bull-ring, currently being converted into a leisure and entertainment centre by Richard Rogers (b. 1933). The park is arranged on two levels. The lower section is green and verdant, separated from the upper part by a long pergola, liberally festooned in late spring with climbing roses. There is also a shady grove of palm trees, which overlooks basketball courts and football pitches. The gentler sporting aspirations of the older members of the community are provided for by a sandy bowling alley, where the most popular games are *petanca*, the local variant of the popular Provençal game *petanque*, and a curious Catalan version of skittles, which features nine Gaudí-esque wooden spires that have to be knocked down by a wooden ball thrown underhand.

The upper part of the Parc Joan Miró is completely paved, with a flat, square pond (currently waterless) out of which rears the monumental *Dona i Ocell* (woman and bird, 1982, left), a work by Joan Miró (1893–1983). The sculpture was installed in 1983, and is covered in red, yellow and blue ceramic fragments called *trencadís*.

Parc de l'Espanya Industrial

The Parc de l'Espanya Industrial, which sits next to Sants train station (the city's biggest mainline station), fits neatly into its ultra-modern surroundings. It was designed by the Basque architect Luis Peña Ganchegui (1926–2009), and is laid out on a site once occupied by one of the vast textile factories that once earned Barcelona the nickname 'the Manchester of Spain'. Stone steps, which also serve as seats, surround the small artificial lake and canal, where boats can be hired. Ten arresting light towers stretch along the walkway at the top of the steps, culminating in the city's largest representation of Catalonia's patron saint, Sant Jordi (St George, c. 275–303). Here he is spearing his dragon in a lively metal sculpture (right) by Andrés Nagel (b. 1947),

which incorporates a slide that is very popular with children. On the other side of the lake, young trees are growing in the lawns among an assortment of contemporary sculptures, and there are courts for squash and basketball. A new sports hall is also planned.

Palau Reial de Pedralbes & Gardens

On the other side of the Avinguda Diagonal from the main University campus, a beautiful park ascends in gradual terraces (below) up towards the Palau Reial de Pedralbes (Pedralbes Royal Palace, *see* pages 134 and 136–37). This leafy paradise was once part of the

country estate of the Güell family, who showed their gratitude for a number of noble titles by donating the estate to the Spanish royal family, to be used as their official residence during visits to Barcelona. The house was handsomely remodelled, and the lavish three-storey building, in the Italianate style, was opened in time for the first visit of the Spanish monarchs in 1926. It did not get many years of royal use before the Spanish Republic was declared in 1931 and King Alfonso XIII (1886–1941) fled to France. The ground floor, with the throne room and large adjoining rooms, is now used for public functions. Upstairs, there is a wonderful collection of ceramic art, with exhibits from the thirteenth to the

nineteenth centuries, as well as a museum of decorative art, which includes a good collection of contemporary Catalan design, featuring chairs, coffee machines and other furnishings. The beautiful, carefully tended terraced park (*see* pages 132, 133 and oppposite), with its many old cedar and lime trees, was designed by Jean-Claude Nicolas Forestier (1861–1930), the much-travelled French landscape architect who laid out the gardens of the Champ-de-Mars below the Eiffel Tower, and also worked extensively in the Americas, spending five years in Havana. A delightful little fountain, designed by Gaudí and featuring a dragon's head of forged iron, was rediscovered by chance during clearance work in the gardens in 1983.

Jardins de la Vil·la Cecília & Amèlia

Two pretty gardens are now open to the public in Sarrià, not far above Plaça Maria Cristina on the Avinguda Diagonal. They are set on either side of a residential street, the Carrer de Santa Amèlia, and used to be the private gardens attached to two of the district's grandest villas. The Jardins de la Vil·la Cecília (Gardens of the Villa Cecilia, left) offer an intriguing maze of tall hedges and lofty palm trees, and a small ornamental canal featuring the statue of a drowning woman. Opposite are the Jardins de la Vil·la Amèlia (Gardens of the Villa Amelia, right and below), equally green but more traditional in layout. They house Sarrià's Civic Centre, with a café-bar and function room.

COL·LEGI DE LES TERESIANES

The Col·legi de les Teresianes is a private school founded for a community of nuns from the Order of Saint Teresa of Jesus, which takes its name from St Teresa of Àvila (1515–82). Construction of the college had already begun when Antoni Gaudí took over the project in 1888. The severe brick façade of the exterior is adorned with neo-Gothic pointed arches along the top storey, but the interior is altogether gentler and more serene. Particularly famous is the upper corridor, where the repeated parabolic arches in white stone create a magical effect. Compared with the unbridled imagination that characterized most of his other commissions, the Col·legi de les Teresianes gives an impression of restraint; Gaudí was a pious man who evidently respected the discipline of the holy order, as well as a businessman who was guided by the constraints of his commissions – at the start of his career, anyway.

RONDA DEL GENERAL MITRE

The Ronda del General Mitre winds its leafy way through the southern reaches of the Sarrià district between the apartment blocks of affluent Barcelonins. As everywhere in the city, there is much evidence of carefully detailed and creative planning of the urban space. The central reservations are attractively landscaped and planted with trees, and there is room for a generous cycle lane. Where its extension, the Gran Via del Carlos III, joins the Avinguda Diagonal at the Plaça Reina Maria Cristina, there is also room for roller-skaters to join in the fun.

BOOMTOWN BARCELONA

By the mid-nineteenth century, when Barcelona was once again enjoying a commercial boom, the city was ready to burst out of the traditional confines of its medieval walls. The gridded new town of the Eixample is as impressive now as when it was first laid out. Its two great avenues, the Avinguda Diagonal and the Passeig de Gràcia, are reminiscent of the grand boulevards of the capital cities of Europe, including Baron Haussmann's Paris. During the period of the Eixample's creation, there was a wonderfully fruitful synergy between the newly rich industrialists and a group of outstanding Modernista architects. The architects vied with each other to produce the most striking and forward-looking designs, while their wealthy patrons competed to outspend their rivals.

Gràcia, named after a long-destroyed monastery, was a peaceful village until the new Passeig de Gràcia linked it with the city. Although now very much part of Barcelona, it retains much of its small-town charm, with a warren of narrow one-way streets interrupted by small squares lined with shops and cafés. Neighbouring Vallcarca is the hilliest of Barcelona's suburbs; visitors to the Park Güell, laid out by Gaudí (1852–1926) for his most important client, Eusebi Güell (1846–1918), will find locals as well as visitors using the escalators that have been provided to help them negotiate the precipitous streets of the area.

PARK GÜELL

The Park Güell, one of Gaudí's most outstandingly expressive creations, was born from a more prosaic premise than one might expect. His biggest client, Eusebi Güell, had the idea of creating a housing development on a hill, then popularly known as the Muntanya Pelada (roughly translated as the 'peeled mountain'), which boasted excellent views across the city. He wanted to emulate the fashion, current in England at the time, for a residential garden city, a self-contained suburb for the wealthy, which would incorporate a coherent design for the public areas. The original plan was to sell off the plots so that the houses themselves would be designed by other architects. The idea never took off – perhaps because it was too far from the city, perhaps because it was too radical – and the Güell family donated the park to the city in 1922.

A Fairytale Place

Little of the original concept has survived, although the English spelling of its name gives a faint clue to its beginnings. Whatever Gaudí's views on the commercial viability of the project, the architect allowed his imagination free reign and, inspired as always by the structural forms of nature, did his best to integrate the design with the surroundings.

Park Güell is a truly fairytale place, and the wonderful exuberance of Gaudí's imagination is breathtaking. When the park was first finished, the visitor was welcomed by two life-sized mechanical gazelles – a typically bizarre religious reference by Gaudí to medieval Hebrew love poetry – although these did not survive the Civil War. The two gatehouses (previous pages and right) that do still remain were based on designs the architect had made for Humperdinck's opera *Hänsel und Gretel*, one of them featuring a red and white mushroom for a roof.

Photogenic Features

The first things that catch the eye are the garden's iron gate and the enormous staircase that leads into the park. The stairs are decorated with waterfalls and sculptures

depicting animals, the most popular of which is a small, multicoloured dragon (left), entirely covered with brightly coloured mosaics – the subject of many thousands of photographs taken each day. Before reaching the main area of the park, the stairs emerge at an open hall, originally intended to function as the main marketplace. Here, 84 tree-shaped pillars twist their way up from ground to ceiling (left and below); in typically Gaudí fashion, form and function are of equal importance and they are as remarkable for their extravagant decoration as they are for their structure. The spectacular space is reminiscent of the hypostyle hall in Luxor. Directly above the market hall is a huge circular terrace trimmed with an immense concrete bench that snakes deliciously round the periphery (*see* page 153). It blazes colourfully with a mosaic of shattered tiles, a technique called

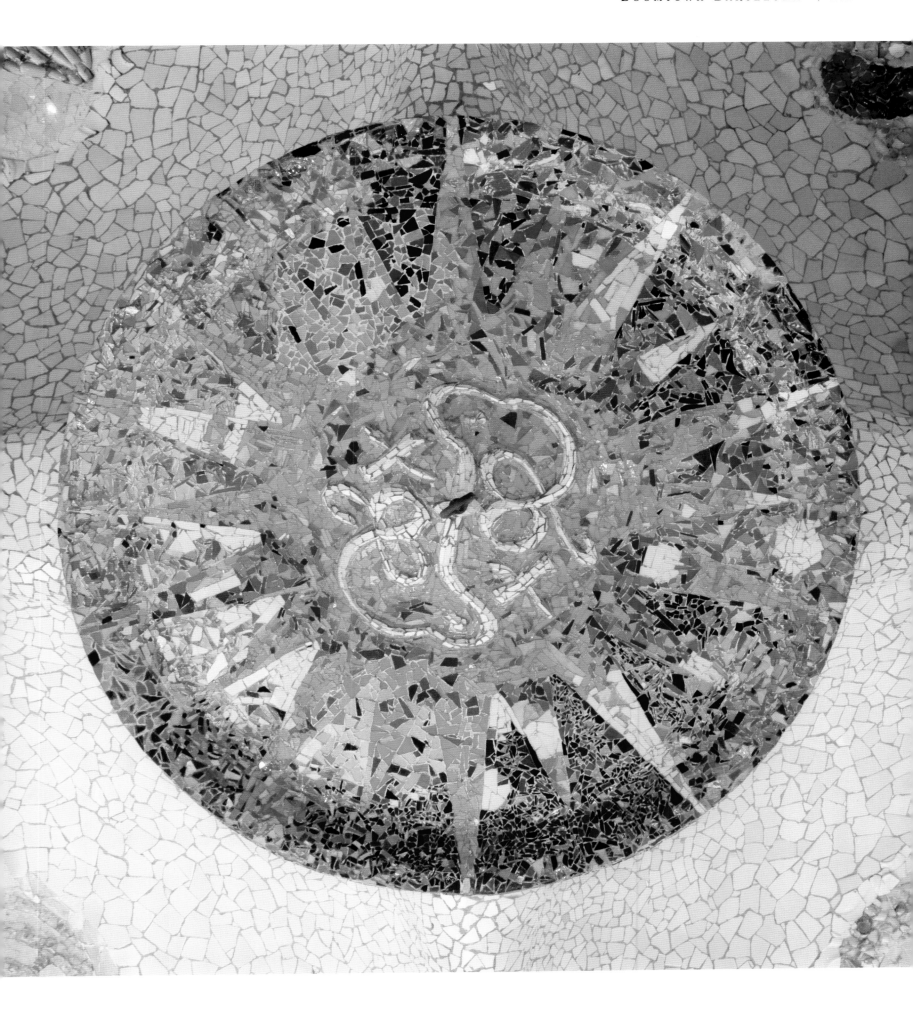

trencadís. Gaudí's overshadowed but talented assistant, Josep Maria Jujol (1879–1949), was a master of this technique, and created this much-loved, much-used, and much-photographed feature.

World Heritage Site

The park is now designated a UNESCO World Heritage Site, and attracts sufficient funding to ensure that it is well maintained despite the wear and tear from the five million tourists who visit every year. Not all make it to the park's peak, which is marked by a large cross and offers an amazing panorama of Barcelona and the sea beyond. Gaudí lived for a time in a rosy pink house (left) designed by his student Berenguer, which contains a good collection of memorabilia from his life.

It can be more rewarding to discover the beauty of Park Güell without the thousands who trundle up here every day to keep one company, so choose a quiet time to head up the hill if possible. Many intrepid aesthetes have been known to come here after a night's partying, to watch the sun come up over the city from one of its finest vantage points. Park Güell is without doubt the most extraordinary monument to Gaudí's soaring imagination.

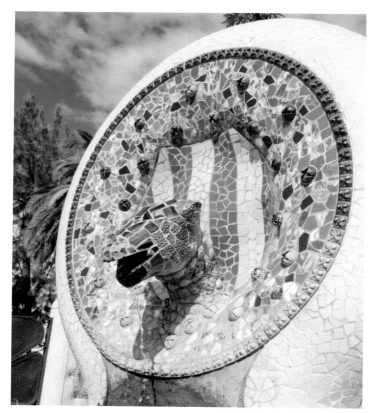

VALLCARCA

Visitors who have trained on the tame gradients of Pedralbes and Sarrià may find themselves unprepared for the serious business of ascending further into the foothills of the Collserola range, which borders Barcelona to the west. This is especially true in the district of Vallcarca, or, to give it its full name, Vallcarca i Els Penitents. Anyone who emerges from one of Vallcarca's two metro stops and heads uphill towards Gaudí's Park Güell will quickly form their own idea of where the 'Penitents' comes from. Luckily Barcelona's city fathers have installed some escalators to help the five million annual visitors reach the entrance of the park

in a fit condition to climb the rest of the hill. If the escalators are out of order, the best advice is to let discretion be the better part of valour, go back down to the main road and find a bus (number 24), which will drop you right at the entrance gate.

CASA TERRADES

At the height of the explosion of Modernista design and architecture in Barcelona around the turn of the twentieth century, there were a fair number of architects vying for commissions and attempting to outdo each other in the flamboyance of their work. And yet they seem to have coexisted in quite an amiable artistic coterie. One of the most sociable architects was Josep Puig i Cadafalch (1867–1956), who was to design the interior of the tavern Els Quatre Gats, that convivial and important gathering place for the Modernista artists. In the Casa Terrades, Puig i Cadafalch took the Gothic and medieval obsessions of the Modernista movement to extremes that others seldom dared. This imposing, castle-like structure, built between 1903 and 1905, was nicknamed the *Casa de les Punxes* ('House of Spikes') because of the needle-like spires rising up from conical turrets (left). The apartment block has the added distinction of being the only fully detached building in the Eixample.

PALAU DEL BARÓ DE QUADRAS

Across the Avinguda Diagonal from the Casa Terrades is another work by the same architect, Josep Puig i Cadafalch, who worked on both buildings at the same time. The Baró de Quadras commissioned Puig to refurbish a residential block on the corner of Carrer Rosselló. It is an extraordinary confection of architectural styles: on one side, a neo-Gothic palace (right); on the other, a Modernista residential block (below). But there is a sound reason for its split personality: each of its two facades were designed to be as impressive as the other, as the building is squeezed into a site between two equally important streets. This arrangement gives the visitor a choice of approaches, each of which creates its own stunning effect.

Fantastic Facades

Most eye-catching is the Gothic side, where Puig built a projecting first-floor window richly decorated in the neo-plateresque style. This name means 'in the manner of a silversmith' (*plata* means 'silver' in Spanish) and describes an ornate style that is more usually found in Seville or Granada. Here the decorations include a wonderful menagerie of mythical creatures, including George and his dragon, the work of that tireless sculptor of the period, Eusebi Arnau (1863–1933). In keeping with

the medieval European theme, busts of eminent medieval and Renaissance figures are interspersed with floral motifs and heraldic shields. The mansard windows on the top story were intended to continue the same noble theme, but to most observers they look just like the windows of an Alpine chalet.

The façade on the other side of the building, overlooking Carrer Rosselló, retains some elements of the original building, reinterpreted in the Modernista style, with some elements of the Viennese Secession thrown in.

Interior Delights

The decor inside is similarly eclectic. Modernista decoration predominates, with the clear influence of the neo-Gothic style on the main staircase (below) and the wrought ironwork at the entrance. Many details, such as the mosaics, sgraffito work and multicoloured woodwork, are reminiscent of the neo-*Mudéjar* style, which recalls Islamic art.

There is also a strong Oriental theme, appropriate for the current occupants of the building, the Casa Asia. This cultural centre celebrates the relationship between Spain and the Asia-Pacific region. The centre hosts a variety of temporary exhibitions upstairs, which provides a welcome opportunity to explore the fascinating building. Many of the rooms have kept the original fittings specified by Puig, including some wonderful stained glass windows that fill them with a soft, coloured glow.

LA PEDRERA

La Pedrera (also known as Casa Milà), the giant apartment block situated on the corner of the Passeig de Gràcia and the Carrer Provença, is Gaudí's most emblematic creation, and one of the most imaginative buildings in the history of architecture. Many consider it more of a sculpture than a building, and believe it embodies Gaudí's imagination at its freest and most whimsical.

Fluid Space

Gaudí disregarded dissenting opinions from other architects and builders, and ignored the serious differences that arose between himself and his client, Senyor Milà i Camps-Segimon, while remaining true to his own ideas. He used La Pedrera to introduce his concept of the *superfície lliure* ('free surface area'), which stipulated that master walls should be eliminated, and structural support should be derived from pillars and partition walls. This meant that the distribution of rooms could be changed freely, easily and as often as desired. This is the premise from which this magnificent piece of abstract architectural sculpture was created, a piece all the more original for the complete absence of straight lines.

The architect created an astonishing building, set out around two oval interior courtyards that provide the flats with ventilation and light. Curved, sinuous forms are the main elements inside and outside the building. The facade resembles the moving sea, the waves interacting with the seaweed motifs on the wrought-iron balcony railings.

Open for Public Viewing

La Pedrera was declared a UNESCO World Heritage Site in 1984, and now belongs to the bank Caixa Catalunya, which has taken on the responsibility for its upkeep. Three areas are open to the public: a reconstructed Modernista flat on the fourth floor, all its rooms preserved and filled with period furniture, including a sumptuous bedroom suite (below) by Gaspar Homar (1870–1953); the attic, framed by parabolic arches worthy of a Gothic cathedral, which also contains a museum offering an illuminating overview of Gaudí's career; and the magical rooftop.

Inspiration on High

Stroll around the roof of the building amid its *trencadís*-encrusted ventilation shafts (overleaf), and you will notice how they are shaped like the helmets of medieval knights

– an abstract motif taken literally in some of the more modern sculptures that adorn the facades of the Sagrada Família. A walk up here also rewards the visitor with beautiful views across the city, up the wide boulevard of the Avinguda Diagonal, and to the Sagrada Família in the distance to the northwest.

This building is one of the high points of Gaudí's career. He was working within the limitations of a commission to design a modern building tailored to modern social needs, but never lost sight of his main sources of inspiration: nature and organic forms. The creative tensions this doubtless inspired, together with the struggles that dogged the building's construction, must have been considerable. After this commission Gaudí never worked on another secular building, pouring all his spiritual and creative energies into the Sagrada Família.

Controversial Beginnings

During the construction of La Pedrera, the building aroused passionate controversy; when it was completed in 1912, it was so far ahead of its time that Roser Segimon, whose husband had financed it, promising her the home of her dreams, became the laughing stock of her social set. The man in the street did not have a much higher opinion of the building, giving it the disparaging nickname 'La Pedrera' (Catalan for stone quarry). Its rippling facade led local painter Santiago Rusiñol (1861–1931) to quip that a snake would be a better pet than a dog for the inhabitants of the building. It seems extraordinary to today's visitor to imagine the storm of adverse opinion that greeted the first appearance of what is now such an emblem of civic pride.

AVINGUDA DIAGONAL & CARRER DE PAU CLARIS

The Avinguda Diagonal was a key feature in Ildefons Cerdà's (1815–76) rationalist grid plan for the Eixample. It quickly proved popular, providing an ideal setting for the new bourgeoisie, as well as the Catalan aristocracy, to display their wealth by parading in magnificent carriages. The building plots, some of them presenting new scope for architectural fancy by their irregular shapes, were quickly snapped up. Eclectic taste was the order of the day, as demonstrated here (left), at the corner with Carrer Pau Claris, named after a proclaimer of the Catalan Republic, Pau Claris i Casademunt (1586–1641).

FUNDACIÓ ANTONI TÀPIES

This intriguing building was one of the first Modernista works to be designed by Domènech i Montaner (1850–1923), which explains why it has so few of the ornate decorative touches that distinguish his later works. It now houses the Fundació Antoni Tàpies, established in 1984 by Barcelona's most celebrated living artist of the same name. Architects Roser Amadó (b. 1944) and Lluís Domènech Girbau (b. 1940) originally renovated the building in 1990, with Tàpies topping the structure with *Núvol i Cadira* (Cloud and Chair, 1990), a monumental sculpture made up of a huge tangle of aluminium tubing and metal netting, which resembles a three-dimensional pencil drawing (below).

CASA BATLLÓ

In eight exciting years, between 1898 and 1906, three adjacent houses in one block on the most fashionable stretch of the Passeig de Gràcia were built to designs by the three great stars of Barcelona's architectural firmament: the Casa Amatller (designed by Puig i Cadafalch), the Casa Lléo Morera (designed by Domènech i Montaner, *see* pages 182–83) and Gaudí's famous Casa Batlló. All three were designed in a different interpretation of the Modernista style, and it must have seemed at the time that they were spurring each other on in what appeared to be a true battle of the giants.

Mançana de la Discòrdia ('apple of discord') was the nickname locals took from Greek mythology to apply to the three buildings, a pun on the word *mançana*, which also means 'block'.

A Modernist Transformation

Despite the grandeur of its two neighbours, Gaudí's Casa Batlló is by far the most expressive. The original house, dating from the 1870s, was bought in 1900 by the textile manufacturer Josep Batlló i Casanovas, who commissioned Gaudí to tear down the old house and reconstruct a new one. Gaudí, however, convinced Batlló to remodel the existing building. Between 1904 and

1906, Gaudí redesigned the facade and roof, added an extra floor and completely refashioned the interior. All the defining elements of the Modernista movement are visible here, especially on the amazing facade, whose ornamental structure seems to have detached itself completely from any received principles of architecture.

Colour, Whimsy and Flourish

Gaudí covered the entire sandstone facade and much of the roof with his classic polychrome *trencadís* (a Catalan mosaic technique). He used wrought iron in whimsical shapes on the balconies, and in decorative elements in

the building's interior. The first-floor windows are bordered by swirling shapes, some of which suggest plants, others entrances to caves. Above these, the facade is covered with glazed ceramic tiles in shimmering green, blue and ochre.

Attention to Detail

The chance to explore the interior offers an excellent opportunity to examine how Gaudí miraculously combined the visionary with the practical. As in his next (and last) commissioned private building, the Casa Milà (La Pedrera), he paid great attention to detail when designing the wooden doors, stained-glass windows, colourful tiles and carved fireplace. He also thought up the ingenious ventilation system for the doors, and designed special brass window handles, curved to fit the shape of a hand precisely. He also created a perfect play between light and colour in the windows, with the sensitive use of stained glass, which gives the spaces inside the building a very magical quality. The wave-shaped roof has, like that of La Pedrera, several richly decorated chimneys.

Access All Areas

One of the apartments inside is open to the public, and access has also been granted to the attic and roof terrace; the whitewashed, arched rooms of the top floor, originally used for laundering and hanging clothes, are among the master's most atmospheric spaces, reminiscent of his Col·legi de les Teresianes in Sarrià.

The house's interior is as fascinating as its exterior. Again, Gaudí flies away from the conventional notion of a room having to be a regular cuboid, and there is hardly a straight line in the whole place. Apparently, his client's wife was worried during the construction process because, according to the design, there wasn't enough space for her daughter's grand piano. Gaudí was too preoccupied to remember her wishes until after the house was completed, when he realized too late that Senyora Batlló had been right to worry. The grand piano could not be fitted in – so he told her, the story goes, to forget about the piano and buy a violin.

CASA LLEÓ-MORERA

The Casa Lleó-Morera (left and below) stands on the southern corner of the block known as the *Mançana de la Discòrdia*. An earlier building was completely remodelled between 1902 and 1906 by Domènech i Montaner (who created the opulent Palau de la Música Catalana) and a team of outstanding Modernista artists, including the sculptor Eusebi Arnau and the stained-glass artist Gaspar Homar. Unfortunately, the most extravagant decoration was destroyed when the ground floor was transformed into a luxury fashion boutique in the 1980s (Salvador Dalí bought the discarded sculptures and installed them in his museum in Figueres), but the architect's whimsical imagination is still apparent in the swirling decoration that adorns the upper levels.

PASSEIG DE GRÀCIA

The Passeig de Gràcia (right and overleaf) was once a humble country lane that linked the city of Barcelona to the separate village of Gràcia. During the 1820s, it was widened into a handsome, elegantly proportioned avenue and became a popular place to stroll and parade in carriages.

The Passeig was among the first of Barcelona's grand avenues to reach its current stately size. But its popularity – both as an escape from the city into the countryside around Gràcia, and as a newly desirable address for the grand mansions to which the rising industrialists aspired – created a demand to which the new Eixample scheme was a response.

In 1906 the architect Pere Falqués i Urpí (1850–1916) designed the avenue's now-famous ornate benches and street-lights. By that time, the Passeig de Gràcia was Barcelona's most fashionable street, and architects, supported by their wealthy clients, vied with each other to create new buildings, each more astonishing and flamboyant than the last.

Nowadays, this avenue is one of Barcelona's most important shopping and business areas. In terms of the cost of renting or buying property, the Passeig de Gràcia is now the most expensive street not just in Barcelona but in all of Spain, outstripping even the glossy Calle Serrano in Madrid.

SOUTHWESTERN BARCELONA

The wooded headland of Montjuïc looks out over the modern docks and huge ferry port below. This quiet, shady hill has long provided a cool retreat for the citizens of Barcelona. Although the hill is mostly occupied by parks and gardens, it also boasts a smattering of grand buildings erected for the 1929 Universal Exhibition. The centrepiece is the enormous Palau Nacional, now the Museu Nacional d'Art de Catalunya (National Museum of Catalan Art).

More monuments were added for the 1992 Olympic Games. The Anella Olímpica (Olympic Ring) includes two vast sports arenas, swimming pools and a

museum dedicated to sports. Stunning views over the city can be enjoyed from the Castell de Montjuïc, a fortress built in the eighteenth century. The stiff climb to the summit is enjoyable exercise, or you could take the funicular from Paral·lel metro station, which links up with the newly refurbished cable car. Close by is Poble Sec ('dry village'), so called because it had no water supply until the nineteenth century. Its narrow streets attract an alternative, arty crowd. The peaceful barri of Sant Antoni is centred around a Modernista market building, dating from 1888.

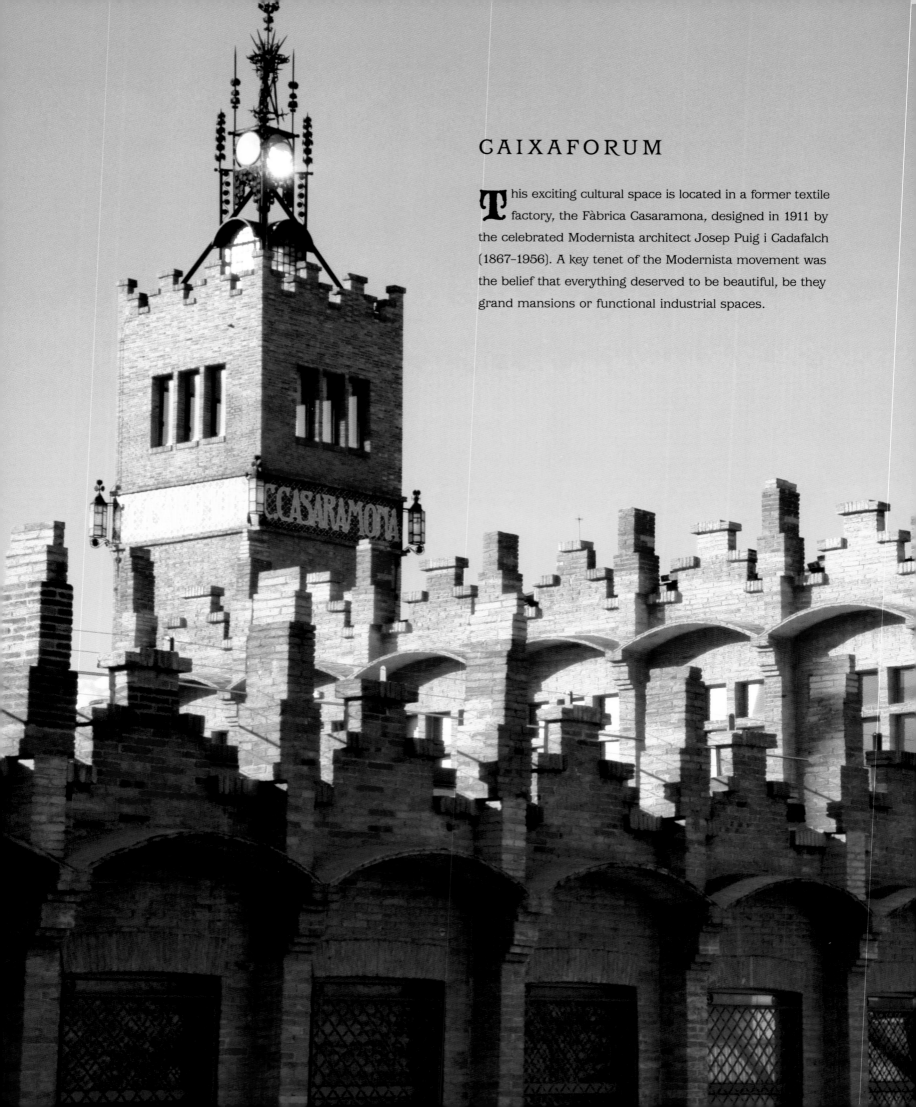

CAIXAFORUM

This exciting cultural space is located in a former textile factory, the Fàbrica Casaramona, designed in 1911 by the celebrated Modernista architect Josep Puig i Cadafalch (1867–1956). A key tenet of the Modernista movement was the belief that everything deserved to be beautiful, be they grand mansions or functional industrial spaces.

The building was on the point of collapse until recently, when Catalonia's largest savings bank, the Fundació Caixa, came to the rescue.

The original brick structure remains intact, but the Japanese architect Arata Isozaki (b. 1951) was commissioned to add a striking modern extension below street level. A wide square at the entrance is decorated with a sculptural element in the form of trees, and a vast, colourful mural by Sol LeWitt (1928–2007) decorates the lobby.

The CaixaForum contains a permanent contemporary art collection, as well as three impressive spaces for temporary exhibitions. Visitors can also explore the old brick towers, which are used for conference rooms and workshops.

MIES VAN DER ROHE PAVILION

ies van der Rohe (1886–1969), one of the foremost exponents of modern architecture during the twentieth century, designed the German Pavilion for the 1929 Universal Exhibition in Barcelona. It was a landmark event in twentieth-century art, and the city has always welcomed innovators. A painstaking reconstruction of the pavilion was carried out in the 1980s, so that future generations could enjoy this perfect encapsulation of his genius.

The pavilion is a sleek geometrical construction of glass, steel and marble overlooking a shallow pool. It epitomizes the ideals of the modern movement in architecture: perfect symmetry, open-plan spaces, precise distances and minimalism. The effect is complemented by Georg Kolbe's (1877–1947) beautiful sculpture, *Alba* (Dawn), which is reflected in the pool, the marble surfaces and the glass, giving the impression that it is multiplied throughout the space. Inside are examples of van der Rohe's celebrated *Barcelona Chair*, which was designed for the Pavilion, and is now an icon of modern design.

MUSEU NACIONAL D'ART DE CATALUNYA

Fans of Jean de Brunhoff's *Babar* books may experience a sense of déjà vu as they look up the Avinguda de la Reina Cristina towards the huge Palau Nacional, which crowns the hill. The elephant king arranged his public buildings in a prominent position on a hillside, but it has to be said that restraint and understatement were more in evidence in Celesteville than they are here. True, the mighty Palau Nacional was intended to impress – it was built for the 1929 Universal Exhibition, together with the pair of Italianate towers (which echo Venice's Campanile di San Marco) that usher in the visitor from the Plaça d'Espanya.

Behind the bombastic facade of the palace, it is a very pleasant surprise to find that what is now the Museu Nacional d'Art de Catalunya has been sympathetically refurbished by the Italian architect Gae Aulenti (b. 1927), and contains an extremely satisfying and important collection of Romanesque, Gothic and Renaissance art. In recent years, the museum has refurbished an extra floor to exhibit the superb Thyssen-Bornemisza collection that was previously displayed in the Monestir de Pedralbes, along with a fine collection of Modernista art and furnishings from the former Museum of Modern Art in the Parc de la Ciutadella.

Romanesque Collection

The most exciting part of the museum is undoubtedly the Romanesque collection. This is a great chance to see some magnificent frescoes, carefully transferred from the many churches in the Catalan Pyrenees that were in danger of falling into ruin. Vaulted ceilings and apses from the original buildings have been exactly reproduced in order to provide a perfect backdrop for the beautiful frescoes. Copies of the original artworks have been installed in the mountain churches. Photographs, ground-plans and drawings accompany the exhibits. In one of the best displays, two apses, from the churches of Sant Pere de Burgal and Santa Maria d'Àneu, face each other. Another highlight is the outstanding *Crist de Taüll,* an

enormous depiction of Christ in Majesty from the twelfth-century church of Sant Climent de Taüll. Even 'graffiti' scratchings (probably by monks) of animals, crosses and labyrinths have been preserved. The museum has recently added a thirteenth-century Romanesque mural, from the cathedral at La Seu d'Urgell, to its collection.

Gothic Art

The galleries displaying Gothic art from the fourteenth and fifteenth centuries are arranged thematically rather than chronologically. There is plenty of work from elsewhere in Spain, although there are many carvings and paintings from local churches, including masterpieces by the leading lights of the Catalan Golden Age, Bernat Martorell (1390–1452) and Jaume Huguet (1412–92). Also on display are stone sculptures and exquisite altarpieces, including the fifteenth-century *Retaule de la Virgen*, probably by Pere Serra (*fl.* 1357–1406). Among the most outstanding works in the museum is Lluís Dalmau's (*fl.* 1428–61) *Virgen dels Consellers* (1445).

FUNDACIÓ JOAN MIRÓ

oan Miró (1893–1983) was passionate about his native Barcelona, and enthusiastically supported the city's cultural life. In 1971, he established the Fundació Joan Miró and asked his long-term friend Josep Lluís Sert (1902–83), another Catalan, to design the building in a prime spot on Montjuïc.

Sert was living in Paris when he designed the Spanish Republic's pavilion for the Paris World Exposition of 1937. The Spanish Pavilion was located right next to the German Pavilion – an unhappy coincidence, as Spain was suffering through the Civil War and the Nazis had just bombed the town of Guernica with the collusion of Franco. Miró was one of the artists that Sert brought in to decorate the Pavilion, along with Alexander Calder (1898–1976) and Pablo Picasso (1881–1973). Picasso's contribution was the famous painting *Guernica* (1937). Sert spent the years of the Franco dictatorship as Dean of the School of Design at Harvard University, but rose to

the occasion for his old friend and created here one of the world's great museum buildings.

Brilliant Showcase

Like Sert's celebrated building for the Maeght Foundation in Provence, which was completed in 1964, this construction is approachable, light and airy. It is formed of a series of cubic elements in gleaming white concrete (*see* page 198), which are illuminated within by semi-circular skylights. The luminous galleries house a collection that comprises more than 225 paintings, 150 sculptures and all of Miró's graphic work, plus some 5,000 drawings. The permanent collection makes wonderful use of the white space to show off Miró's exuberant use of primary colours and sensuous organic forms. An added attraction is Alexander Calder's reconstructed *Mercury Fountain*, first created for the Spanish Pavilion in Paris in 1937.

ANELLA OLÍMPICA

The Anella Olímpica (Olympic Ring), a group of sports and entertainment facilities that occupies the upper reaches of Montjuïc, was the main focus of the 1992 Olympic Games. One of the main facilities was already in place: a giant stadium built for the 1929 Universal Exhibition, which was remodelled in the 1930s

when Barcelona first bid to host the Olympic Games. An anti-fascist 'People's Olympics' was organized here in protest after the 1936 Games went to Hitler's Germany. Many of the participating athletes had actually turned up in Barcelona, when, on the day before the Games were due to begin, Franco's military revolt sparked off the Spanish Civil War. Many athletes stayed in the city to sign up with the Republicans.

For the 1992 Olympics, the seating capacity of the stadium was increased to 70,000, and the fine original exterior, with its eclectic mix of styles, was renovated. Renamed in honour of Lluís Companys (1883–1940), the heroic former president of Catalonia who was shot by the Nationalists after the Civil War, the stadium is now home to one of Barcelona's football teams, FC Espanyol.

Iconic Structures

The spectacular exterior of the Palau Sant Jordi, a sports arena by Japanese-born architect Arata Isozaki, could not be more different from that of the nearby Olympic Stadium. Isozaki wanted to echo the shape of the hill, as well as give Barcelona a new symbol whose form would contrast with the strong verticals of the Sagrada Família and the towers of the Museu Nacional d'Art de Catalunya, with which it shares the skyline of Montjuïc. The shallow dome of the roof consists of a giant metallic web combined with glazed ceramic tiles, drawing inevitable comparisons with a flying saucer.

A stronger vertical could hardly be imagined for the Palau's near-neighbour; the spectacular design of the communications tower (left) by Valencian architect Santiago Calatrava (b. 1951) became one of the symbols for the 1992 Barcelona Olympics.

CASTELL DE MONTJUÏC

The Castell de Montjuïc, sitting at the very top of the hill, commands tremendous views over the city. It was designed as a coastal battery to protect the docks and harbour below, but was used more often to attack the city than to defend it. In just one incident, in 1842, General Espartero (1793–1879) controlled a riot by bombarding the centre with over 1,000 shells, which destroyed more than 400 buildings. The castle has the further unhappy distinction of having been used for much of its existence as a political prison and execution ground. Many anarchists were killed here at the end of the nineteenth century, and, during the painful aftermath of the Spanish Civil War, the Nationalist authorities tortured and killed tens of

thousands of Republicans within these grounds. Among them was the President of the Catalan government, Lluís Companys, in whose honour the football stadium has been renamed.

Peace Centre

The castle was finally handed over to the city in 2008, but until then it remained in state control. In the past, it has been used as a military museum, containing portraits of most of the monarchs who have attempted to repress Catalonia, and a diorama of the detested fortress of Ciutadella, which was built to subdue the restive Catalans in the eighteenth century. The city authorities have decided to turn the castle into an International Centre for Peace, which, one hopes, will put to rest some of the ghosts that lurk here.

POBLE SEC

The little warren of streets at the bottom of Montjuïc, which also borders the seamier southern reaches of El Raval, goes by the name of Poble Sec, 'the dry village'. As mentioned, the name has nothing to do with strict views on liquor, but came about because it was last area of Barcelona to be supplied with mains water. The wide Avinguda del Paral·lel, which slices between Poble Sec and El Raval, got its name as far back as 1794, when one of the city's astronomers spotted that it lay exactly along the line of the latitude 41° 44', a curious fact that has always fascinated the Barcelonins, whose city refuses to line up to a measure as mundane as north–south (the visitor to Barcelona should remember that the map they are looking at is unlikely to be arranged to the points of the compass, and is more likely to have the coast neatly ranged due 'south'). The metro stop Paral·lel is the start of the enjoyable funicular up to Montjuïc. Next door is a popular skateboard park in the shadow of three huge chimneys, striking relics from Barcelona's industrial past.

SANT ANTONI

Sant Antoni is one of the most relaxed districts in Barcelona. The quiet community is centred around the beautiful covered market of Sant Antoni, which opened in 1882. It is almost as large as the famous Boqueria on the Rambla, but considerably less frantic. While major restoration works are carried out (part of a city-wide regeneration project that has seen several of Barcelona's neighbourhood markets elegantly remodelled), the produce stalls occupy a huge tent just outside the original building. Another recent source of pride is the Sant Antoni public library, a sleek creation in black glass, which is found half a block away from the market. The entrance, imposing yet subtle, leads to an ultramodern courtyard and playground, where a light-filled centre for senior citizens has also been incorporated into the design.

NORTHERN & EASTERN BARCELONA

Barcelona is constantly renewing itself, and most districts have experienced dramatic change. In the northwest of the city, the Horta neighbourhood was once open fields and orchards. Many of these were part of great noble estates, some of which were later transformed into pleasure gardens. Perhaps the finest of these was owned by the Marquès de Llupià i d'Alfarràs, who established the exquisite park that would later become the wonderful Parc Laberint d'Horta in 1791.

The Eixample district is divided in two by the Passeig de Gràcia: the southern section is known as the Left Eixample (L'Esquerra de l'Eixample) and the northern section is the Right Eixample (La Dreta de l'Eixample). The Right Eixample is dominated by the enormous and still-unfinished church of the Sagrada Família, which became the great obsession of Antoni Gaudí's (1852–1926) later

years. Construction work is privately funded, from donations and the income from admission tickets. Although its soaring spires look set to share the skyline with cranes for some time yet, it is hoped that the Sagrada Família will be complete in time to celebrate the hundredth anniversary of Gaudí's death in 2026.

The old working-class district of Poblenou spreads north of the Eixample along the coast. This neighbourhood has seen extraordinary changes in the last couple of decades, particularly during the run-up to the 1992 Olympic Games and for the Universal Forum of 2004. Locals may complain that they are being ousted from their old neighbourhood as the development money pours in, but they certainly seem to enjoy the new open spaces, particularly the pleasant, remodelled Rambla de Poblenou.

PARC DEL LABERINT D'HORTA

Most of Horta, once a rural district at the foot of the Collserolla hills above the city, is now densely built up, with a mixture of apartment blocks, colleges and sports facilities. The award-winning Velòdrom (cycle track), designed in 1984 by Esteve Bonell (b. 1942), is worth a peek, but the real jewel of this neighbourhood is found just a short stroll up the hill behind it. From the Velòdrom, a footbridge crosses the road and leads up to the formal gates of a landscaped garden laid out on the hillside. This was created by Joan Antoni Desvalls (1740–1820), the Marquis of Llupià and Alfarràs, an enthusiastic supporter of the new fashion for formal landscaping during the Enlightenment in the late eighteenth century. He conceived of a garden on the themes of Love and Disappointment, and hired Italian architect Domenico Bagutti (1760–1837) to design the layout. The garden was set around a cypress maze and filled with romantic streams and waterfalls.

Amazing Maze

The original summer residence was built beside a medieval watchtower, the Torre Soberana, which survives in romantic ruins. The main house was replaced in the

nineteenth century by an Arabesque confection. The park originally encompassed 133 acres, of which only 17 have survived, but they are breathtakingly beautiful. They have remained remarkably intact, shaded in the summer by oaks, laurels and an ancient sequoia. The chief attraction is the maze that gives the park its name, which lies on the lowest of three ascending terraces. Visitors attempt to negotiate a path through the tall cypress hedges to find the tantalizing statue of Eros at the centre.

Donated for Posterity

A balustraded terrace overlooks the maze and serves as a platform for local youths to shout out misdirections to befuddled tourists. On the top level is an ornamental pool and a fine neoclassical temple (right). Other architectural features include sculptures, terracotta jardinières (planters), pergolas, cascades, canals and a hermit's grotto. The gardens became internationally famous and received many royal visits. In the mid-nineteenth century, the marquis's descendants commissioned architect Elies Rogent (1821–97) to extend the grounds, adding a romantic garden with flower beds, small squares, tall trees and a waterfall.

In 1967, the Desvalls family decided that they could no longer keep up the property and donated it to the municipality of Barcelona, which opened the gardens to the public in 1971. Since 1993, the mansion has been occupied by the Centre de Formació del Laberint, the city's Institute for Botanical Studies.

HOSPITAL DE LA SANTA CREU I SANT PAU

The Hospital de la Santa Creu i Sant Pau, with its intricate arrangement of separate pavilions set among attractive gardens, is the most harmonious of projects in the Catalan Modernista style: beautiful and functional at the same time. It was designed by Lluís Domènech i Montaner (1850–1923), who aimed to create a light-filled, open-plan hospital far removed from the grim institutions that were the rule in most European cities at the time.

By the end of the nineteenth century, the original Hospital de Sant Pau in El Raval had become increasingly unusable in its cramped and outdated premises. The outstanding Modernista architect Lluís Domènech i Montaner was commissioned to design new premises for a site in the recently developed Eixample neighbourhood. The new hospital was to be a modern, spacious facility, a miniature 'town' of separate pavilions, connected by streets and surrounded by green areas to stroll in. It eventually occupied more than nine blocks in the northeast corner of the Eixample. The plot was angled at 45 degrees from the rest of Ildefons Cerdà's grid plan so that it could catch more sun. Domènech i Montaner built the hospital on the assumption that patients would recover more quickly when surrounded not just by fresh air and natural light, but also by colour and beauty. Some

of his practical innovations were forward-thinking: a network of underground tunnels, for example, made it easier and safer to move patients between the wards and other departments.

An Eclectic Style

The imposing brick building topped with a clock tower at the main entrance is the hospital reception. Domènech i Montaner and his team (which included the sculptors Pau Gargallo, 1881–1934, and Eusebi Arnau, 1863–1933) let their imaginations run wild on the facades of all the hospital buildings. They mixed and matched from their eclectic palette of Byzantine, Gothic and Moorish influences, with lavish decorations using mosaic, stained glass and sculpture. The octagonal columns with floral capitals are inspired by those of the Monestir de Santes Creus, southwest of Barcelona. The entire complex took 30 years to build, from 1901 to 1930, and the final stages were completed after the architect's death by his son, Pere Domènech i Roura (1881–1962).

World Heritage Status

The Hospital de la Santa Creu i Sant Pau was declared a World Heritage Site by UNESCO in 1997. When part of the roof of the gynaecology department collapsed in 2004, it was clear that restoration work was essential on the century-old Modernista 'garden city' hospital. The last of the medical departments has recently been transferred to the modern building north of the grounds, leaving the old complex to an uncertain future, although there are tentative plans to turn part of it into a museum dedicated to the works of the Catalan Modernista architects.

LA SAGRADA FAMÍLIA

Antoni Gaudí's extraordinary fantasy, the Sagrada Família – or, to give it its official name, *Temple Expiatori de la Sagrada Família* (the Holy Family Church of Atonement) – has dominated the city's skyline for almost a century. From the moment Gaudí became involved in the plans for the church, it was destined to become the most unconventional church in Christendom. It is certainly the most famous sight in Barcelona and draws millions of awestruck admirers from all corners of the world. Considerable patience is required during the high season when queueing for tickets, but the entrance charge is going towards a worthy cause – no less than the completion of this mighty work, which receives no state funding.

A Life's Work

When Gaudí was put in charge of constructing the church in 1883, plans had already been drawn up and work had begun on the construction of what was originally conceived as a church in the Neo-Gothic style. Gaudí decided to change the plans completely but, as was the case with almost all his work, had no firm ideas in mind, preferring to alter and add to the designs as work progressed. Of course, this meant that the project would take time (although Gaudí had originally forecast that construction would take between 10 and 15 years). There were also financial limitations, as the cost was to be met solely from donations and public subscription. After the death of his chief collaborator, Francesc Berenguer (1866–1914), Gaudí gave up the rest of his architectural practice (his last commission was the Park Güell) and devoted himself obsessively to the building of the church. As the work dragged on, support dwindled, but for Gaudí this had become a holy cause. He dedicated the rest of his life to the church's construction, eventually selling his house and possessions and moving into a hut on the building site.

The Work Continues

Gaudí's obsession with the project continued until his untimely death in 1926, after he was hit by a tram while crossing the Gran Via. But he had managed to complete the crypt and the great Nativity façade by this time, and the huge scale and brilliant inventiveness of the design ensured that the project was not abandoned. Gaudí left some models and drawings, which have made it possible for building work to continue. Enthusiastic collaborators include the architecture departments of Barcelona's university, the University of Deakin in Australia and the University of Wellington in New Zealand. At present they are hard at work calculating the possibilities of building the transept without buttresses, in accordance with Gaudí's original concept (he considered buttresses 'crutches'). He was always a great admirer of the organic forms of nature, and, as his work at the Park Güell illustrates, often took inspiration from the ways in which trees support their own great height and weight.

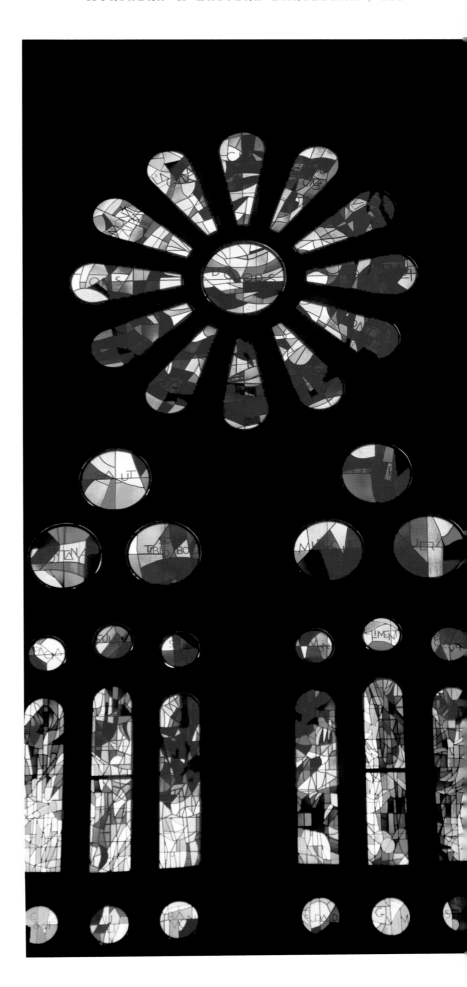

Symbolic Building

Every element of the Sagrada Família symbolizes something. The eastern facade is dedicated to the Nativity (*see* page 228 and right), the western one is dedicated to the Passion of Christ (*see* page 230), and the Glory facade, which is the biggest of all, is devoted to religious faith. The four towers on each of the three facades represent the 12 Apostles. A dome-shaped tower will eventually crown the apse, symbolizing the Virgin Mary, and the central spire, representing the Saviour, will be built over the crossing, one-and-a-half times the already-dizzying height of the surrounding four towers dedicated to the evangelists. Anyone with a good head for heights can queue for the elevator that rises to the top of one of these towers, where thrilling, if vertiginous, views of the church and across the city can be enjoyed.

TEATRE NACIONAL DE CATALUNYA

The Plaça de les Glòries Catalanes was part of Ildefons Cerdà's (1815–76) original scheme for the Eixample, although it was never fully developed during his lifetime. Until recently, in fact, it has been nothing but a large roundabout where arterial roads meet. But this area of eastern Barcelona is now the focus for the city's latest phase of regeneration. An iconic landmark already draws the eye: Jean Nouvel's (b. 1945) cigar-shaped Torre Agbar (far left). Its distinctive silhouette takes its inspiration from the rocky forms of the mountains at Montserrat. The first new building of the scheme was inaugurated in 1997: the spectacular Teatre Nacional de Catalunya (these pages). Its striking design, by Ricardo Bofill (b. 1939), is a post-modern rendition of the Acropolis in Athens.

ESGLÉSIA DE LES SALESES

The decorative church of the Salesians (below) was commissioned in 1878, and completed and consecrated in 1885. It is a beautiful pre-Modernista building in which Gothic, Romanesque and *Mudéjar* styles are successfully combined. It is considered the finest work of Catalan architect Joan Martorell i Montells (1833–1906), a disciple of Viollet-le-Duc (1814–79). Martorell is most famous for having taught Antoni Gaudí, who later worked as his assistant.

PARC DE L'ESTACIÓ DEL NORD

The alternative name for this popular park (right) near Barcelona's main bus station, the Estació del Nord, is *Parc Sol i Ombra* (Park of Sun and Shade). The park incorporates a sculpture by American artist Beverly Pepper (b. 1922) entitled *Cel Caigut* (Fallen Sky, 1986), which is clearly inspired by Gaudí. Its wavy form is covered in sky-blue mosaics, which form a beautiful contrast with the green grass and inspire peaceful meditations in those who come to the park to relax.

PARC DE LA CIUTADELLA

The Parc de la Ciutadella now provides a precious 'green lung' right in the city centre, but it has a long and sometimes painful history. During the War of Spanish Succession in the early eighteenth century, the Catalans allied themselves with the Austrians against the Bourbons. In 1714, after a long siege, Barcelona fell to the troops of King Philip V of Spain. He decided to punish the Barcelonins by closing down the university, and ordering the destruction of a great swathe of the old city. In its place rose a huge pentagonal fort named the Ciutadella, which kept an eye on the citizens of Barcelona from very close quarters. (It later proved an ineffective defence, and was quickly taken by the French in 1808 during the Napoleonic Wars.) Finally, in 1869, a popular Catalan, General Prim (1814–70), ordered that it be dismantled and the area turned into a park.

Universal Exhibition

In 1888, the mayor of Barcelona chose the Parc de la Ciutadella as the main site for the city's Universal Exhibition. The architect Josep Fontseré (1829–97)

adapted the 18-hectare park to the needs of the
exhibition, and many of the buildings built specially for it
are still visible today. Domènech i Montaner designed the
Castell dels Tres Dragons (previous pages), one of the
city's earliest Modernista edifices, to house the Exhibition
restaurant. It now contains a section of the Museu de
Ciències Naturals (Natural Science Museum), with another
in the restrained neoclassical edifice nearby. This is

flanked by two more survivors of the 1888 Exhibition: the *Umbracle* (Palm House) and *Hivernacle* (Winter Garden). Nearby, you can see a replica of Josep Llimona's (1864–1934) beautiful Modernista sculpture *El Desconsol* (Distress, 1940), one of the most important pieces of public art in the park. Also of some interest is the Palau de Justícia (below), by the architects Enric Sagnier (1858–1931) and Josep Domènech Estapà (1858–1917).

Arc de Triomf

The main access gate to the 1888 exhibition was the monumental Arc de Triomf (far left), which dominates the Passeig Lluís Companys and provides a splendid approach to the park. The gateway was designed by architect Josep Vilaseca i Casanovas (1848–1910), who envisioned a modern interpretation of the Roman triumphal arch built of red brick in the then-fashionable neo-*Mudéjar* style. A grand frieze by Josep Reynés (1850–1926), *Barcelona Rep Les Nacions* (Barcelona Welcomes the Nations, 1887), adorns the front of the arch. On the other side, the celebrated Modernista sculptor Josep Llimona contributed an early work, a carved frieze entitled *Recompensa* (Reward, 1891). The top of the arch is decorated with carvings by Torquat Tassó and Antoni Vilanova, representing the Barcelona coat-of-arms and symbols of all the Spanish provinces.

DIPÒSIT DE LES AIGÜES

The Universitat Pompeu Fabra (UPF), Barcelona's new public university, was established in 1990. Many of its most important buildings are on the new Ciutadella Campus, which makes imaginative use of some of the monumental nineteenth-century buildings that line the northern side of the Parc de la Ciutadella. Among these is the University's largest library, the Dipòsit de les Aigües, which makes brilliant use of a

water tower originally designed in 1874 by Josep Fontserè. A young student of architecture named Antoni Gaudí was in charge of some aspects of the study that accompanied the commission. The final design was an updated copy of a Roman prototype. The building has been put to many different uses in the last century, including a stint as the municipal asylum and another as a changing room and garage for the local police, but since 1999 it has provided an original but perfect home for the university's library.

POBLENOU

Barcelona's city-planners are now waving their magic wands over the once-neglected and down-at-heel former industrial quarter of Poblenou, which is currently undergoing a massive urban renewal programme. The southern swathe of the district was transformed into the glossy waterside developments of the Vila Olímpica and the Port Olímpic for the 1992 Olympic Games. The Universal Forum of Cultures in 2004 provided an excuse to remodel the northern section, where the coastline meets the Avinguda Diagonal, into an area now called

Diagonal Mar. A huge shopping centre and a clutch of four- and five-star hotels have opened up here. The Edifici Fòrum, centrepiece of the 2004 event, was designed by Jacques Herzog (b. 1950), the architect responsible for London's Tate Modern gallery. The entire development is conceived on a giant scale, and the modest residential district of Poblenou, which runs north–west from here, seems a little dwarfed. However, the procession of cranes that are transforming the cityscape, block by block, suggest that change is both fast-moving and inevitable. Much of Poblenou's former industrial heritage is currently being

converted into a commercial zone for high-tech and digital businesses, named 22@Barcelona. It also already has a landmark, the intriguingly shaped Torre Agbar (*see* page 236), designed by Jean Nouvel, who is responsible for much of the neighbouring development. A new tram line links Diagonal Mar with the Plaça de les Glòries.

Cementiri Vell

It is to be hoped that the many charming corners of old Poblenou will escape the wrecking ball. One that is likely to survive is the much loved *Cementiri Vell* (old cemetery, previous pages), peacefully enclosed behind high walls that shut out the hubbub of the new seafront just a few steps away. Trim rows of family tombs are stacked neatly near the entrance, the plastic floral tributes lending a macabre air of permanent gaiety. Further into the cemetery, wealthier families lay their dead to rest in semi-detached or even detached premises, often wonderfully ornate, encrusted with sorrowing angels and spanning a bewildering range of architectural styles. One of the most histrionic sculptures is worth searching out: the statue of *El Bes de la Mort* (the kiss of death), in which a skeleton forces his attentions on a marble youth.

Contrasts

Not far from the entrance of the cemetery is a complete contrast, a civic project very much of the twenty-first century that seems to have gone down well with the local residents. This is the delightful Parc del Poblenou, also designed by Jean Nouvel. His idea was to isolate the park visually and acoustically from the traffic, using walls of flowers. There are several separate sections, including a square for dancing the Catalan *sardana*, and the old Oliva Artés factory, now the Barcelona Architecture Centre.

One of Poblenou's most charming and traditional avenues remains central to local life: the Rambla del Poblenou (right). For a long time, this was the only rival to its glamorous namesake in the city centre, until the new Rambla del Raval was built a few years ago. It is a pleasant mix of shops, cafés and apartment blocks, with a sprinkling of Modernista buildings and plenty of good places to sit under the shade of plane trees.

INDEX